be your o

For Dean,

With love
+ hugs,

Olivia
xxx

be your own **guru**

personal and business enlightenment in just 3 days!

olivia stefanino

CAPSTONE

First published 2007 by Capstone Publishing Ltd. (a Wiley Company)
The Atrium, Southern Gate, Chichester, PO19 8SQ, UK.
www.wileyeurope.com
Email (for orders and customer service enquires): cs-books@wiley.co.uk

Other Wiley Editorial Offices
John Wiley & Sons Inc., 111 River Street, Hoboken, NJ 07030, USA
Jossey-Bass, 989 Market Street, San Francisco, CA 94103–1741, USA
Wiley-VCH Verlag GmbH, Boschstr. 12, D-69469 Weinheim, Germany
John Wiley & Sons Australia Ltd, 42 McDougall Street, Milton, Queensland 4064, Australia
John Wiley & Sons (Asia) Pte Ltd, 2 Clementi Loop #02–01, Jin Xing Distripark, Singapore
129809
John Wiley & Sons Canada Ltd, 22 Worcester Road, Etobicoke, Ontario, Canada M9W 1L1
Wiley also publishes its books in a variety of electronic formats. Some content that appears in
print may not be available in electronic books.

A catalogue record for this book is available from the British Library and the Library of Congress.

ISBN 13: 978-1-84112-727-8
ISBN 10: 1-84112-737-X

Typeset in Adobe Garamond 12/15pt by Sparks – www.sparks.co.uk
Printed and bound in Great Britain by TJ International Ltd, Padstow, Cornwall

This book is printed on acid-free paper responsibly manufactured from sustainable forestry
in which at least two trees are planted for each one used for paper production. Substantial
discounts on bulk quantities of Capstone Books are available to corporations, professional
associations and other organizations. For details telephone John Wiley & Sons on (+44) 1243–
770441, fax (+44) 1243 770571 or email corporatedevelopment@wiley.co.uk

For Paul

xxxxxxssxxxxxx

Contents

What it means to be your own guru   xi

How to get the most from this book   xiii

Introduction   *The Banker*   1

Section 1   Me! Me! Me!   7
                   Until you know who you are, how can you
                   know what kind of life you want to live?

Chapter 1   Meeting the delegates   9

Chapter 2   Why most training simply doesn't work   12

Chapter 3   Jenny dumps her emotional baggage   19

Chapter 4   Why healing the past is the only way
                   to guarantee a great future!   33

Chapter 5   Pete turns stress to his advantage   45

Chapter 6   Getting to the real cause of stress   50

Chapter 7   Matt discovers the childhood reason
for his shaking hands   54

Chapter 8   Learning to deal with negative emotions   64

Section 2   **Free! Free! Free!**   79
*When you know that you're more than just
a physical body, you've got a real head start in life*

Chapter 9   Discovering the amazing power
of the subconscious mind!   81

Chapter 10   Getting to grips with what makes you tick   89

Chapter 11   Experiencing the mind/body connection   111

Chapter 12   Using your body to read your mind   121

Chapter 13   Learning to talk the talk   129

Chapter 14   Watch your language   136

Chapter 15   Death is our teacher   143

Chapter 16   It's only when you can face death
that you're ready to live   151

Chapter 17   Are you simply a figment of your imagination?   157

Chapter 18   Are you the product
of your history or your potential?   164

Section 3	**You! You! You!**	**171**
	Until I understand you, and you understand me – how can you and I create 'WE'?	
Chapter 19	Different views, same world	173
Chapter 20	It's our differences which make life so exciting	180
Chapter 21	Using intuition and energy to create phenomenal relationships	189
Conclusion	The Banker announces the results for the pilot project	203
Afterword		207
Section 4	**Tools! Tools! Tools!**	**209**
	Gathering knowledge isn't power – applying knowledge is power	
	Tools to be your own guru	211
	The Self Journey (using PEAR)	218
	The Relationship Journey (using PEAR)	221
	The Soul Journey	225
Index		229

What it means to be your own guru

When you discover how to be your own guru, you'll be happier, healthier and wealthier – guaranteed!

You'll also have an innate wisdom that others will find irresistible, which means that your relationships – both at home and at work – will grow stronger, more meaningful … more delightful!

And as both your personal power and intuitive awareness expand, you'll find that life begins to unfold much more easily as at last you find yourself at 'cause' rather than 'effect' in your life.

How to get the most from this book

Be Your Own Guru has been written to appeal to both your imagination *and* logic – which is why you'll find both a true story (the odd numbered chapters) and the rationale behind it (the even numbered chapters) running throughout the book.

Using all of your brain in this way guarantees that you'll not only make sense of what you're reading but you'll also intuitively grasp the bigger picture too. But understanding on its own isn't enough. It's equally important that you're able to apply your new-found knowledge – which is why you'll find a whole section devoted to the tools you'll need to help you on your journey.

DISCLAIMER

None of the exercises or tools in this book are intended to replace professional advice or therapy. If you feel it's necessary, you must visit a medical professional to deal with any physical, emotional and psychological problems.

Introduction
The Banker

*I*t had just gone half past two on a cold, wet February afternoon when the telephone rang, interrupting the silence.

'OK', said the deep voice with the unctuous quality of molten chocolate, 'Here's the deal …

'We're interested in your programme but you have to prove that it works. And not just in the short term. In fact, we want to evaluate the results over a nine month period. Interested?'

Of course I was interested. I was more than interested. I was ecstatic. 'So how are you going to measure the results?' I asked, in as cool a voice as I could muster.

'Well, we're going to split the region's senior business banking team into two groups – half will come through your programme and the rest will form a control group for comparison. And I'm afraid we're not going to be fair. We're going to give you the people who just don't seem to be performing *to the levels we expect. They have the knowledge and experience alright, but for some reason they just don't seem to be measuring up against their colleagues – even those colleagues who've only just started working at the bank. Anyway, the plan is that at the end of the nine month period, we'll measure your group's sales results against their previous performance and against the control group.*

'Oh, there's one more thing. You only have three days to run your programme.'

With the conversation over, the phone clicked and the line went dead.

Jubilation and terror struck in equal measure. The optimist in me was ecstatic at the thought that I could prove my programme in a scientific and credible way. The pessimist in me, however, could see that failure at this juncture would put a stop to my second career before it had even started …

The dark, chocolaty voice belonged to an individual whose career in banking was so important to him that many suspected he'd already sold his soul to further his ambitions. It was hard to warm to him – and yet, I had to give it to him, he had courage. Not everyone would have been prepared to put their neck on the line to give me an opportunity. But it wasn't until later that it began to dawn on me that my banker wouldn't have risked his own neck if he didn't think he was on to a winner.

We'd met through a mutual contact nearly six months previously and during that time we established a relationship based on a shared interest in what makes people tick. Recognising right from the start that he had a particularly robust ego, I'd chosen to call him 'The Banker', a title that somehow seemed to sum him up perfectly and which, to be fair, he appeared to enjoy.

Even though his aloofness was a little off-putting, he did have a particularly dry sense of humour which I took a perverse pleasure in provoking.

Expecting me to run the programme in just three days was hardly playing by the Queensbury Rules. In fact, it was damn ridiculous. I wondered whether I'd have made a better judgement call if I'd turned down his offer. But that wasn't my style – all my life I'd enjoyed being challenged by the seemingly impossible and this wasn't an opportunity that was likely to come around more than once. I simply needed to work out how I could achieve the impossible in three days!

The Banker later admitted that he was attracted to my programme because of the results it promised. He also liked the fact that in my previous career I'd been a journalist – which had given me a pretty sceptical outlook on life. He knew that I wouldn't put my name to something that wasn't credible – and in the past we'd both enjoyed poking fun at some of the 'pink and fluffy' personal development ideology that had seemed so popular at the time.

Return on investment was the key to success in The Banker's eyes and I was always careful to talk to him in those terms. 'Profits are the measure of success for every company. And I don't care what anyone says about the importance of looking after your staff – unless there's a measurable improvement to the bottom line, it's a waste of time. At the end of the day, companies measure success in terms of increased profits.

'Millions get spent annually on "touchy feely" people development', he said, 'but most of it's simply a waste of time. Companies like to think it makes them look good – but in my opinion the fact that each year there's a new training fad suggests that most of it simply doesn't work in the long term.'

And, in a theatrically conspiratorial voice, The Banker then added – to my dismay – 'If you want to know the truth ... I think most trainers are simply ... parasites!'

Opening his mouth to continue his diatribe, The Banker suddenly paused – remembering that I earned my living as a trainer of sorts. Perhaps out of kindness but more likely out of embarrassment, he abruptly closed it again – swiftly aborting the rest of the torrent that was about to flood out.

After a few moments silence, I smiled and said, 'Actually, for the most part, I agree with you.'

Saying nothing, The Banker's left eyebrow merely rose in surprise.

'A lot of trainers I've met don't seem to measure the effectiveness of their work.' I continued, 'It's almost as though everyone is paying lip service to training and simply going through the motions.'

'Quite', he muttered, carefully removing a piece of fluff from his sharply pressed trousers.

I continued, 'I've often wondered why companies seem to spend so much time and energy dealing with the symptoms of their "people problems" without taking the trouble to get to the cause. It's rather like western and eastern medicine. In the west, we're fantastic at dealing with accidents and emergencies – but in the east, the doctors seem to be more interested in keeping people well rather than waiting until they're ill!'

I cited the old system of Chinese medicine in which the village doctor is paid the equivalent of a few pennies by each family to keep them well. 'As soon as someone is ill, the doctor stops getting paid. But when you think about it, in the west, our doctors only get paid when we're ill! Where's the incentive to keep us well?'

The Banker smiled at the analogy.

'I think looking after employees has to take the same approach.', I said, warming to my theme, 'At the end of the day, it comes down to personal leadership. For me, until someone feels connected to the "higher purpose" in their life, they're never going to really put their heart and soul into their work. It's about so much more than just goals – it's about having a personal vision, and then knowing how to align that vision with the requirements of the employer. Equally importantly, there's all too often a heap of emotional baggage that simply gets in the way of an individual's success – and until it gets dealt with there's no room for new learning, let alone improvement.'

As our conversation drew to a close, The Banker and I touched upon our mutual dislike of the 'groupie' mentality which seems to surround certain 'big names' in the personal development world. 'Surely', I said, 'the point is to invite people to be their own guru, rather than have to rely on someone else to provide all the answers?'

'That certainly would seem the best way to enlightenment', The Banker replied drily.

Section 1

Me! Me! Me!

*Until you know who you are,
how can you know what kind of life you want to live?*

Chapter 1
Meeting the delegates

*T*hree days to achieve the impossible wasn't long – but in my favour I'd managed to negotiate with The Banker that each of the delegates should have access to the equivalent of three days of my time. I'd also managed to persuade him that the days could stretch into the evening as well. This gave me a little leeway. My plan was to have a pre-course two-hour session with each delegate, followed by a two day training session – reinforced with three individual coaching sessions every two months. It was going to be tight but I was confident I could do it.

The Banker had invited the nine business managers he'd selected to be in my training group for coffee in the boardroom. As The Banker and I waited for them to arrive, I wondered how things would pan out. In the middle of my musings the door opened to reveal Jenny, a shy slim woman with a mousy bob who looked as though she was in her early 30s. She gave me a quick half-smile and limply shook my outstretched hand.

'Hello', she said, 'can I pour you a coffee?'

The words were only just out of her mouth when the others started walking in through the door. The Banker had been true to his word: 'my' group of business bankers really were a mixed bunch.

As well as Jenny, I felt an immediate bond with two of her colleagues. Pete was the eldest of the group and while he had a somewhat cynical air about him, there was a twinkle in his eye which made him attractive, in a 'favourite uncle' sort of way. My attention was also drawn to Matt, a serious young man with a dark mop of hair that was slicked back with a more-than-generous helping of gel.

After we'd all got our coffee, we sat down at the massive, highly polished oak table and waited for The Banker to begin. He spoke only briefly, first introducing me and then going on to outline the parameters of our pilot project and how its effectiveness would be measured. As I looked around the table, I could see a mixture of reactions. The younger ones, Matt in particular, looked interested and pleased that they had been selected. Jenny studiously looked down at the table, twiddling with a small tendril of hair. Pete had the air of one who'd seen it all before but he was too polite to let his scepticism be revealed to any great extent.

With the formal introductions over, it was now time for me to explain how the project would run. 'I have just three days', I said, glancing over at The Banker, 'and we've got to cover a lot in that time. First of all, each of you will be having a two-hour session with me …' A snigger erupted from the far end of the table. Ignoring it, I continued, 'The purpose of the session is threefold. First of all, it will give us an opportunity to get to know each other; secondly, it will help me tailor the two day leadership course and thirdly and most importantly, it will give you an opportunity to take some time out for you to think about you! Oh, and of course I should say that all of our one-to-one sessions will be completely confidential.'

'Sounds more like a therapy session to me', laughed Matt.

'Yes', I replied with a half smile, "for some people the first session does become like a therapy session and I make no apology for that. Everybody's session

will be completely different but from previous experience, I guarantee that you won't find it a waste of time!'

I knew there wasn't much to be gained from labouring the point – they'd have to see the value of the sessions for themselves. I spent the next five minutes explaining how the two day personal leadership course would focus on 'self mastery' and 'relationship expertise'.

'Following on from the two day training programme, you'll each have an opportunity for three follow-up coaching sessions every two months – happy with that?'

Everyone nodded their head and, with the slightly cynical part of me coming to the fore, I wondered if they'd agreed to take part in the programme simply as a way of getting out of the day job.

'We've no time to lose – so I'm proposing that we start the initial sessions straight away. Who wants to go first?' I asked, looking around the table.

Suddenly the gleaming shine of the French-polished table seemed to be of paramount importance, judging by the deep inspection it seemed to be soliciting from the delegates. Much to my surprise – and as I was later to find, to hers – Jenny put up her hand saying, 'Me, I'll go first.'

Chapter 2
Why most training simply doesn't work

Harvard University law professor Derek Bok once said that 'If you think training is expensive, try ignorance' – and no one would argue that continuous personal and business development is a must in an increasingly fast-changing world. However, with profits still remaining the measure of success for most companies, excellent return on investment for training activities is a 'given'.

Sadly, training has become something of a dirty word in many organisations – mainly because historically, it's represented a poor (or at least, unmeasured) return on investment. For many companies, simply being able to 'tick' the training box in a human resources audit is enough. But for other, more enlightened businesses, sourcing the kind of staff development that really adds to the bottom line is somewhat akin to the mystical search for the Holy Grail. Of course, training costs come out of profits and not turnover – which is why in hard times training can seem like something of a luxury. When there's a squeeze on profits, the first piggy bank to get raided is the one bearing the 'training' label.

While many companies pay lip service to their 'people' being their key asset, in reality, the over-whelming focus has been on developing those very same 'people' solely to ensure that the organisation achieves its own objectives.

> **Guru Success Tip**
>
> If you want to create change, remember that the people you want to change need to know what's in it for them!

But be warned, the 'people', are beginning to revolt! If you're running a business and you're looking for evolution not revolution, then you'd better cotton on quick to the fact that your staff need – and want – to know what's in it for them. And if you're working in someone else's business, you've still got every chance of attaining glittering success – but only if you're clear about your personal 'purpose' *and* have found a way to align it with the needs of your boss.

While city fat cats continue to coin it and company shareholders revel in their role as the modern gods who must constantly be appeased, all too often the emotional needs – and dare I say it, spiritual needs – of employees are simply overlooked. But if we – at all levels – are to put our hearts and souls into our work, we need to know that as well as achieving the work targets set for us, we're also able to fulfil *our own* aspirations at the same time. In other words, for any of us to feel that our work has meaning, we need to see that our employment not only fits into the 'bigger picture' of our lives but that it can also pave the way to manifesting our dreams.

While you may not have had time to stop to think about it, work holds much more significance for us than merely keeping a roof over our heads and food on the table. We tend to identify ourselves through what we do – and if you don't believe me, see where the conversation leads next time you meet somebody new!

We take an interest in what people do for a living, not only because it enables us to find some common ground, but because discussions about what we 'do' become a kind of shorthand. With just this one key piece of information, we're able to sum up the other person's status and ascertain whether or not we have enough in common to make the relationship worth pursuing. Sure, it may not sound politically correct, but nevertheless we all do tend to do it! Sadly, it's also human nature to measure our success against other people – and somehow there's a kind of security that comes with knowing how and where we fit into the social pecking order.

CLIMBING THE SLIPPERY LADDER CALLED 'CAREER SUCCESS' ...

Most of us hope to advance up the 'food chain' at work – so it stands to reason that if we expect to earn more, then somehow or other we must make sure that we're *worth* more. Traditionally, training in the work-place focuses on improving skills, while personal development tends to see more attention paid to attitudes and personal leadership. Most companies tend to invest in training, believing that they need their workforce to become more 'skilled' – but skills are simply the tip of the iceberg. Much more important are habits. And underlying habits are your personal motivations.

> **Guru Success Tip**
>
> What you think about dictates your actions – and your actions dictate your results. So be very careful to think about what you want, not what you don't want!

While to be fair, some corporate training is pretty good – giving you access to some of the best expertise around – much of it is pretty 'grey', leaving you wondering what's for lunch half an hour into the first morning session! Personal development, however, is harder to come by in the workplace. Because it's less easy to measure in terms of return on investment, fewer organisations regard it as a priority.

But there's nothing stopping *you* from investing in *your* future. Who else has a greater interest in how your career pans out than you? If you were the HR director in your life, how would you go about developing you? You're responsible for your career – not your boss, not your parents and not your peers. It all comes down to you.

Taking charge of your *own* career – as I discovered when I worked in journalism – is the only way to grow. In order to progress I had to create my own 'promotion ladder' by applying for jobs that were outside my comfort zone but which stretched me far more than sitting passively, waiting for my dream job to come along!

Sometimes it helps to think of yourself as being self-employed, which when you stop to think about it you are – irrespective of what the taxman might have to say about it! (The only difference between working for a company and being freelance is the number of clients you serve. When you're employed, you technically have only one client – your employer, who pays your salary. And when you're self-employed you have a number of clients, who each – in effect – contribute part of your salary.)

WHY YOU OWE IT TO YOURSELF TO FIND YOUR UNIQUE PATH ...

Each of us has something unique to offer the world – and it's through this unique offering that we all get to serve each other, creating a Utopian world of 'interdependence'. And just so we're clear here, serving others doesn't make you servile. ('Service' suggests work done by one or more people to the benefit of others while 'being servile' suggests being something of a servant and in a subordinate position.) We're all here to serve – no matter which rung of the career ladder we're on.

> **Guru Success Tip**
>
> Poor leaders expect to be served and demand respect ...
>
> Great leaders expect to serve and earn respect!

Discovering your soul purpose, the unique offering that you bring to the world, is simpler than you think – and you probably already have an intuitive knowing about your 'mission' for this lifetime, even if you can't quite yet see how to make it practical and income generating! Your soul does nudge you along the way as your gifts tend to arise out of whatever makes your heart sing …

Sometimes, it's about nothing more than giving yourself 'permission' to be the very best of who you are. Or, in other words, it's about making the decision to lead your own life, rather than give your power away to other people, who are often only too happy to adopt the leadership role in your life! Sadly, it's all too easy to listen to the people around you and be put off from pursuing your life's real purpose. While – hopefully – family and friends probably do want what's best for you – the likelihood is that they'll project their hopes, fears and beliefs on to you. If your parents, for example, grew up with little spare cash, then their overwhelming belief is likely to be that you must go into a 'safe, well-paying' career. Now, that might well satisfy their needs, but will it satisfy yours? Equally disappointing is the fact that not all your friends and colleagues will want you to succeed either – fearing that your successes will show up their failures.

If you want to achieve lasting success and happiness, choose to spend your time with like-minded people. Have you ever noticed how gossipers tend to flock together, picking over other people's misery like vultures picking over the remains of a dead animal? Intriguingly, I was once advised by a friend not to walk away from negative people. It had seemed like a strange thing to say until he'd added, shouting at the top of his voice, 'RUN, RUN AS FAST AS YOU CAN!'

WHY YOU ABSOLUTELY HAVE TO HELP YOURSELF FIRST …

Training at work often takes the 'one size fits all' approach, but if you're to become the very best that you can be, it stands to reason that because you're unique your personal development needs to be unique too.

Personally, I think it pays to focus your development on your strengths rather than your weaknesses. It seems incomprehensible to me that in our schooldays, we only receive coaching to help us plug our weaknesses – but all that does is ensure that we all achieve a similar level of mediocrity! Play to your strengths and your weaknesses will take care of themselves. It's a maxim that applies in business – as I finally learned when I gave up the struggle to do my personal and business accounts myself – after several years of growing frustration. Not only had maths never been my strong point but the tedium of counting up columns of figures inevitably used to bring on a migraine. After longer than was good for my sanity, I realised that if I focused on doing what I was good at, I'd be able to afford to pay someone else – an accountant – to do what they excelled at. That way, we all get to do what we love to do – and what needs to get done, gets done! Perfect, abundant, interdependence!

Traditional training tends to focus simply on improving *skills*, but skills are just the tip of the iceberg! Long-lasting improvement only comes about when *habits* are changed. Good habits are the key to effectiveness. However, habits are only changed when there's sufficient *personal motivation*. Will-power alone isn't enough to change a habit. Motivation is the key.

It's about putting the correct building blocks in place – and in the correct order. In order to create the foundations, you're going to have to understand why you do what you do. Do you go to work because:

- You need to keep a roof over your head?

- What you do for a living gives you an identity?

- It's the only way to create the future you've always dreamed of?

Its only when you understand why you do what you do that you can begin to see whether or not you're actually living your life on purpose. Does going to work make you feel excited or do you do you suffer with the Monday morning blues? Interestingly, research has shown that there are more heart attacks on a Monday morning than at any other time during the week!

There's a lot of talk in the personal development world about goals and action plans and while most of it's highly commendable, it can leave you yawning politely behind your hand. But the essence of it is this: Unless you know where you're going, you're going to have a hard time getting there. But once you know what you want out of life, you can use the work you're doing now to create your future.

And frankly, it's only when you and your employer work out how you can both *align* your goals that you both start to get what you want from the working relationship. When you and your boss create a win–win situation in this way, you start working to get the life you want and your boss gets those all important higher profits!

One of the reasons people end up miserable at work is because they feel they have no control over their lives. It's as though we feel that he or she who's the paymaster gets to call the shots. But in reality, we do have much more choice than we think but it's up to us to get off our butts and start working on purpose, our purpose!

Chapter 3
Jenny dumps her emotional baggage

*S*miling in Jenny's direction, I said, 'Well, there's no time like the present. We'll wait for the others to leave and then without further ado, we can get started.'

Jenny had the look of a frightened rabbit caught in the headlights of an oncoming car and it was clear that I was going to have my work cut out just to reassure her. As the door closed behind the last straggler, she looked at me expectantly, wondering what was going to happen. Her face, which was devoid of any make up, looked tired and careworn, as though she carried the weight of the world on her shoulders, which themselves were slightly hunched. She looked like she was seeking refuge from a tough world.

Reaching into my brief case, I pulled out a 'wheel of life' and passed it to her, along with a finely sharpened pencil. As Jenny stared at the piece of paper in front of her, I explained the purpose of the 'wheel' and how she should complete it. On the sheet of paper were ten concentric circles, with the smallest, inner circle being a score of 1, and the outer, largest circle being a 10. Dividing the circles were eight straight lines, with a different topic heading for each.

'All you need to do', I said in a reassuring voice, 'is to think about how you feel about each topic and give it a score out of 10. On this scoring system 1 is low and 10 is high. For example, let's look first at the line labelled Career. If you're delighted with the way your career is going, then you'd give yourself a 10 but if you absolutely hate your work, then you'd score yourself a 1. Of course, you probably won't feel quite so extreme about any of the topics but you get the picture.'

Jenny nodded and picked up the pencil. While there was nothing magical about the wheel in itself, I knew that what it would reveal would make a good conversation starter. Curiously, I'd observed that even the way someone completes the wheel can say a lot about them, a point that Jenny was about to demonstrate perfectly.

After a couple of minutes passed, Jenny put the pencil down again. It was as though she was in deep contemplation, perhaps deciding whether or not to be honest with herself, possibly for the first time in her life. As I was to explain later to her, the interesting thing about tools such as the wheel of life is that because they're visual, they tap into the creative part of the brain – bypassing the logical, rational and judgemental parts.

Picking up the pencil again, she carefully began to mark her scores on the wheel. As she drew the final cross, she sat back in her chair with her eyes firmly fixed on the piece of paper.

'Just one more thing', I said. 'Perhaps you'd like to join the crosses up for me – just like on a dot-to-dot puzzle. It's the only childish thing I'll ask you to do, I promise!'

Jenny nodded, leant forward and was about to begin when she stopped to ask if I had a ruler she could borrow.

'Don't worry', I said, 'there's no prize for how the wheel looks, just do it freehand.'

As Jenny joined the dots up, I smiled inwardly. Jenny's request for a ruler showed me that she had an eye for both detail and neatness. These traits were reflected in her neat suit, sensible haircut and low heeled shoes. Sometimes people filled in the wheels in a very cavalier manner, crossing things out messily and connecting the dots in one untidy swoop. Either way was fine but already it started to give me clues as to the type of personality sitting in front of me.

Jenny's wheel was far from round – in fact it looked very spiky. She had given herself average scores for 'Health', 'Purpose' and 'Family', a high score for 'Career', 'Money' and 'Partner' but low scores on 'Self' and 'Friends'.

'Don't worry', I said, 'most people find that their wheels look a little odd! By the way, did you drive here this morning?'

'Yes. Why?'

'Well, if you think about it for a moment, your car journey was probably pretty smooth because, despite any bumps in the road, the wheels on your car are nice and round.'

Jenny looked at the wheel she'd just completed and smiled – she'd already got the point. Laughing, she said, 'Driving on something shaped like this would have been pretty uncomfortable. I suppose what you're getting at is the fact that the rounder our wheel of life, the more smooth our life journey will be?'

'Exactly', I replied. 'Balance is the key. But then so is feeling good about each area in your life. You could, of course, have a very small but balanced wheel – if you'd given yourself a score of 1 for every element. But with a tiny wheel like that you wouldn't get anywhere very fast!'

'So should we be aiming for a perfect 10?' interrupted Jenny.

'Interestingly, no. A perfect 10 all the way round would suggest that there was no room for improvement – so I think that an 8 or 9 is the score to aim for.' After taking a sip from my glass of water, I turned to Jenny and asked her why she had given her partner a much higher score than she'd given herself.

A nervous giggle escaped from her throat, and Jenny admitted that she hadn't realised that she had created a discrepancy in the relative scores. 'To be honest, I'm really lucky with partner. Not only is he supportive of me but he also has a great job, which is probably why I was able to score highly on my 'Money' line because with his income, finances really aren't a problem for me. I think my partner is cleverer than me – and more successful at work, which is I suppose why I gave him a higher score.'

I noticed that Jenny's throat was beginning to redden slightly, a sure indication that we were hitting on a subject that was difficult for her. 'OK, here's another question for you. Who's the most important person in your life?'

'Oh, that's easy. Phil, my partner. Definitely.'

'And who else?'

'Well, I guess my parents come next.'

'And who else?'

'Well, I'm pretty close to my sister.'

'Great, and who else?'

'Hmmm. Well, I have a couple of close girlfriends …'

'OK, I'll put you out of your misery. The correct answer – and it's the only 'trick' question that I'll ever ask you – is …'

'ME!' Jenny almost shouted, finishing the sentence off with a laugh.

'Don't worry too much', I told her, 'I had one woman once who told me that her most important relationship was with her pet rabbit, so things could be a lot worse!'

Jenny smiled and as she did so, her whole face lit up – making her look almost pretty and certainly less dowdy.

I went on to explain to Jenny that until we recognise ourselves as important, we tend to put others' needs first, which can have disastrous consequences. Seeing Jenny's frown, and remembering my own confusion at the concept, I decided to try to illustrate what I was getting at by reminding her of the safety instructions air stewardesses give before take-off. 'As part of the emergency spiel, they tell you that if the cabin pressure falls, an oxygen mask will be dropped in front of each passenger. And they emphasise the point that you should fix your emergency mask first, before attempting to help anyone else, including your children.'

Pausing for a moment to smile at Jenny, I then continued, 'When I first heard it, I thought it was terribly selfish and almost unnatural. After all, aren't we brought up to help others less able than ourselves? Wouldn't our survival instinct force us to help our children before helping ourselves? But as I'd pondered on it, it suddenly dawned on me that until you get yourself sorted, you become someone else's problem. Perhaps the most important gift that we can give to anyone is our ability to take responsibility for ourselves.'

Jenny had been listening intently to every word. Neither of us spoke for a moment. Jenny was the first to break the silence saying, 'I'd never thought of it like that before. I can see that I've been so busy trying to make things easier for everyone else that I've completely ignored my own needs. I've always thought that if I did all I could to make someone else happy, then they'd want to do the same for me. But in reality, that hasn't been my experience at all.'

'Do you feel resentful, taken for granted?'

Jenny opened her mouth to speak but as tears began to roll down her cheeks, she simply nodded instead.

Passing her a tissue, I reassured her that it was OK to cry. 'Lots of people do in these sessions, you're not the first and you certainly won't be the last. In fact, I recommend to people that if they're going to buy shares they should buy them in Kleenex!'

Laughing through her tears, Jenny took a deep breath and admitted, 'If I'm honest, I've been feeling resentful for a while. I feel like I'm being taken for a mug, both at home and at work.'

Jenny's feelings weren't uncommon. Many people feel they have to 'earn' love in order for friends and family to appreciate them. Without a strong sense of self, people like Jenny often believe that they're not 'good enough' and it's not long before they end up in a vicious twin cycle of martyrdom and victimhood. Although on the face of it, martyrs appear to be prepared to do anything to gain appreciation, you only need scratch the surface to find an unhealthy dollop of manipulation at play. Giving when you're counting the cost isn't really giving at all. It's not long before the receiver begins to recognise that there's a price to pay. Either they choose to ignore the martyr's litany of 'after everything I've done for you' (which makes the martyr turn to 'guilt-tripping' in a bid to get the attention they crave) or they in turn begin to manipulate the martyr, using them to do the stuff that they simply can't be bothered to do themselves. Internalised anger makes the martyr/victim feel even worse about themselves, so once again they begin a vicious cycle of 'people pleasing'.

After explaining my observations to Jenny, she immediately asked if the 'condition' was more prevalent in women.

'I've not measured it scientifically', I responded, 'but anecdotal evidence would suggest that women do indeed tend to fall into this cycle more easily than men. I can only hazard a guess as to why this could be. Perhaps it's because women tend to be brought up to believe that their role is to take care of everyone else – and little girls tend to be rewarded for being sweet and

thoughtful! However, don't run away with the idea that men have a higher opinion of themselves than women. From all the clients I've dealt with in the past, I wouldn't say that this is true at all. It's just that men tend to deal with their fear of personal inadequacy differently. They're more likely to create an air of bravado around themselves, which to some people comes across as self-confidence and to others as arrogance! While the symptoms tend to be different, the root cause of these behaviours tends to be the same – a lack of self love.'

As we were on the subject of self love, I asked Jenny what score she would give for how she felt about herself. 'If 1 is "I hate myself" and 10 is "I love myself," what score would you give yourself? Oh, and I should point out that by loving yourself, I don't mean that you're completely narcissistic – I'm talking about feeling comfortable and at peace with who you are.'

'I'd give myself about a 2 – maybe a 3 on a good day!' Jenny said in a quiet voice.

'OK, that's OK. So, how do you think your life would be if you liked or loved yourself a little more?' I asked.

Hesitating for a moment, Jenny started to smile at the prospect. 'Well, I suppose I'd be happier and more confident. I'd probably care less about what people think of me and do more of the things that I enjoy. In a funny kind of way, I think I'd feel freer!'

'Absolutely', I replied. 'From all that we've said so far, I'm sure you'd agree that the better we feel about ourselves, the happier and more successful we're going to be! So, how about we start to look at the blocks to your happiness?'

'What? Now?' spluttered Jenny.

'Yes, now!' I replied.

'Surely getting to the root of why I don't like myself is going to take a lot longer that one session?'

I shook my head. 'No, I'm sure we can do all we need in this session right now. I guarantee that you'll feel a lot better when we've finished – and you should know that I wouldn't ask you to go through any process that I haven't been through myself many times. Of course, sometimes it's a bit like peeling an onion, once you've dealt with one issue, another one pops up to be healed. But the process we're about to use is so powerful that most issues can be dealt with quite easily in just one session. So, how about we make a start and I'll prove it to you?'

'Sure', said Jenny in a tone of voice that suggested she wasn't sure at all.

After making sure that both our mobile phones were switched off, I invited Jenny to close her eyes and then to take in three deep breaths from an imaginary bubble of white light. As her breathing slowed, I asked her to travel back in time to when she'd first started to feel that she wasn't good enough.

'Tell me what you see', I asked her in a low voice.

Struggling at first to summon up enough energy to speak, Jenny eventually whispered, 'Oh … I can see a picture of my baby brother.' There was a small pause before she continued, 'I'm looking at when he came home for the first time after he was born. He'd been premature and my parents felt that he was special and fragile … and needed to be treated like fine china … My grandparents came round and lots of family friends too … and he was getting all this attention … and no one took any notice of me at all … It was as though I didn't exist … I can see now that before my brother came along, I was the one who was doted on … but it felt as though I was just cast aside after he was born.'

'Move on to the next significant incident with your brother', I directed.

Slowly, Jenny started to speak again. 'I'm about seven now … and I'm being smacked because I'd left him to play on his own when I'd been told to look *after him … He'd run his tricycle into a tree in the garden and had hurt himself … I can see a small trickle of blood running down his face … He wasn't really hurt but he was making such a fuss and I got the blame … as usual. I didn't ask for him to be born … It's not fair.'*

'Good work', I said in a reassuring voice. 'So what's the next significant thing that happens?'

'I'm helping Mummy in the kitchen, she seems to like it when I do things for her … I'm helping her make a cake and then I go on to do some ironing for her … But I burn myself on the hot iron and start to cry … Mummy gets cross with me and tells me that I should have been more careful … She tells me to stop crying and start behaving more like a grown-up … It's not fair, Mummy's always cross with me. Whatever I do, it never seems to be good enough … But she's got lots of patience with my brother.'

Tears started to roll from the corner of Jenny's left eye. Passing her a tissue, I asked her if she'd like to feel better about the whole situation. Looking almost childlike, Jenny began to nod.

'OK, now I want you to get an image of your little brother in your mind's eye. Can you do that?'

A nod was all the answer I needed.

'Excellent. Now, I want you to tell him how you felt as a little girl. I want you to tell him how you were happy until he came along – and how much it hurt when you found yourself no longer the centre of attention. Tell him how angry and unhappy you are – and I want you to tell him all of this out loud.'

I knew that if Jenny was ever to feel better about herself then she needed to let go of the hurt and bitterness she felt towards both her brother and mother. The key to letting go is forgiveness – but the first stage in the process is to express all the anger and hurt, which was what Jenny was now doing.

'I hate you', said Jenny in an ominously quiet voice. 'Ever since you came along, it was as though I ceased to exist ... You've always been the apple of Mummy's eye ... In fact I think she prefers you to me ... And even though we're grown up now, things haven't really changed. Mum is perfectly happy to let you and Dad sit around and be waited on all day but she expects me to look after myself ... I'm sick of it ... I'm just so sick of it.'

More tears came and as they began to subside, Jenny's shoulders dropped and she took in a deep breath. This was a non-verbal cue that she'd got all of the anger and hurt out of her system.

*'OK Jenny, well done. In a minute, I'm going to ask you to forgive your brother but first, I just want you to listen to my words. Forgiveness doesn't mean that you condone someone's actions – instead it's the key to your own freedom. Forgiveness doesn't mean that you give your power away – rather it means that you take your power back. All the time you're holding on to anger and hurt, **you're hurting yourself**, not the other person. Your brother probably has no idea how you feel and has been happily going through life unaffected by your anger. The only person who is affected by your anger is you! So, I'm sure you'll agree that it makes sense to stop giving your power away to your brother in this way. It's time to set yourself free. Forgiveness isn't a decision that washes over you at some point. And despite what you may have heard, time isn't a healer. You know that already, don't you? You've been carrying this anger and hurt around for a long, long time and time hasn't made it go away has it? In fact, the less you feel like forgiving someone, the more you actually need to do it. Does this all make sense to you?'*

Jenny nodded.

'OK. Now, I want you to look your brother in the eye and find something that you can forgive him for. Perhaps you can forgive him for getting you into trouble when he ran his tricycle into the tree?'

Again, Jenny nodded. 'Phil', she said in a very small voice, 'I forgive you for getting me into trouble with Mum ... I forgive you for being Mum's favour-

ite and I forgive you for "doing no wrong" in her eyes.' As she continued through the process, she seemed to find it easier to forgive. As she started to draw to a close, she took a deep breath and then muttered, 'In fact Phil, I choose to forgive you for being born!'

At that, an odd noise had come from Jenny's throat, a curious blend of a sob and chuckle.

'Now', I gently guided, 'make the decision to accept Phil for who he is – and how he is. Know that while he may never change – and that's OK – today you've changed.'

Jenny did so – speaking out loud to the Phil she could see in her imagination.

'Great, now imagine that you're giving him a big hug. I know it might seem like a strange thing for you to do, but you're the one in control now and you can decide what you are – or aren't – going to do. Fantastic! Now, as you look at Phil, you'll see in your mind's eye that he has a gift for you. What is it?'

At first Jenny frowned and then smiled, saying, 'He's got a box, a beautiful dark wooden box which is wrapped with a lovely pink and gold ribbon!'

'That's wonderful. In spiritual circles, pink is associated with love and gold with power; isn't it lovely that the box is wrapped with a pink and gold ribbon?'

Jenny nodded.

'What's inside the box?'

'Oh. Nothing!' Jenny sounded disappointed.

Deciding quickly to reframe the situation for her, I pointed out that 'nothing' was actually 'pure potential' – and that Phil was giving her the gift of inviting her to be herself and create the kind of life of which she had always dreamed!

'That's lovely. I feel a strange kind of peace washing over me.'

'That's right', I said, 'You do.'

Next we repeated the forgiveness process with her mother. It was much quicker, not least because Jenny knew what to expect. The first time, as they say, is always the hardest!

With our work for the session done, I brought Jenny back to an awakened state and she blinked her eyes a couple of times to remove the blurriness. As I looked at her, I smiled, amazed as always at how letting go of emotional pain can bring about a dramatic change in physical appearance. Jenny looked as though she'd dropped ten years from her face – and even she was able to notice the difference, although her face was still a little tear-stained.

'Wow, I feel so much lighter!' she exclaimed, 'but really tired too.'

'That's not surprising', I replied. 'You've been holding on to all of this stuff for a very long time now. When you suddenly let go, it's as though all your muscles no longer have to strain to keep control and as they relax for the first time in ages, you become aware of their fatigue. Don't worry, you'll get over the tiredness pretty quickly – but I can guarantee you an excellent night's sleep tonight!'

Jenny laughed and acknowledged that I was probably right. It was time for her to leave and as she stood up, she started to thank me – going on to give me a spontaneous hug. As she was later to acknowledge, her life was to change dramatically after that session. It was as though being free of so much emotional pain had released an energy within her – an energy that she was now able to use to create the life of her dreams.

Points to ponder as you start to ...
Be your own guru

Success is subjective – you get to decide what success means to you. For some people, success is measurable only in material terms, while for others success means feeling that 'all is well' within the world. While there's no right or wrong, it does help to know 'where you're at' in life – not least so that you can do whatever's necessary to get back on track. Below you'll find the wheel of life – a great tool for measuring how you feel about how you're doing in life.

Wheel of life

Wheel of life diagram with vector lines labelled: Self, Purpose, Health, Career, Money, Partner, Family, Friends. Scale marked 10, 5, 1 from outer to inner.

Wheel of life instructions ...

Taking 1 to be the smallest, inner circle and 10 to be the largest, outer circle (the halfway line is highlighted in dark grey) mark with a cross on each vector line where you feel you 'are' on a scale of 1 to 10. When you have completed this, join each of the crosses together, rather like a dot-to-dot exercise ...

Once you've completed the wheel, it's easy to see at a glance which areas require work – and in which order! Use the exercise as an evaluation tool to see how you're improving over time.

More questions to help you on your way …

1 If 1 is 'not at all' and 10 is 'very', how content are you with who you are, and how your life is going? What would it take to improve your score?

2 Write – or at least think about – your response to the question: 'Who am I?'

3 Think about someone whom you love unconditionally – how do you treat them in comparison with yourself? How would you treat yourself if you loved you unconditionally? Would you be kinder, more forgiving and less critical? Would you be more encouraging, make more time for yourself and simply enjoy life more?

4 After completing the wheel, in which areas do you need to start the goal setting process?

5 As you look back over your life, can you see any patterns that have repeated themselves in the areas of your life in which you have scored yourself low?

6 If you could wave a magic wand, what would your working life look like?

Chapter 4
Why healing the past is the only way to guarantee a great future!

The key to effective personal development is dealing with the emotional baggage we've accumulated. Clearing out the old debris is the only way to make room for new learning.

It's hard to acknowledge but we hurt ourselves far more than anyone else can hurt us. It's the replaying of past hurts in our minds that really causes us the problems – more so than the actual event itself. And if we've buried the memories really deep, we may not even be aware of what it is that is causing us the difficulties. We can only heal our past by bringing it into conscious awareness and then making the decision to put it to rest. Of course, we don't have the ability to change the events that happened to us – but we do have the power to change how we *feel* about those events.

While we may believe that we're in control of our feelings, all too often they are, in fact, controlling us. Festering in our subconscious minds, negative emotions mean that we end up viewing the world through the grey tinted lenses of past experience. And because the subconscious mind stores all our memories – together with the emotions we felt at the time an event occurred – you could even say that we live life as a product of our own history!

Guru Success Tip

Recognise that if you're not in charge of your emotions – then they're in charge of you!

Until we understand and heal our history, we'll always be controlled by it. It's only when we find the courage to face our past and make the difficult decision to let go of any self-righteous negative feelings that we have, that we're free to move into a space where we can create the kind of life we want. That's what it means to be a co-creator. Our journey then, is along a path which leads us from being trapped in the past to being free to create our future.

Understanding this is the foundation to effective personal leadership. At the end of the day, it comes down to *creating a great relationship with yourself*. And before you reach for the sick bag, just stop for a moment and question whether you treat yourself better or worse than other people. We're brought up to put other people first – and yet doing so often creates untold misery. I remember once being at a seminar when the facilitator mentioned the Biblical instruction that 'we should love others as we love ourselves'. And then, almost as a throwaway remark, he'd gone on to add, 'and imagine turning that round for a moment – and loving yourself as you love others!' It was a remark that stayed with me all day and I began to recognise that I was being invited to treat myself with the same compassion and lack of criticism that I endeavoured to show others. It was so simple – by being nicer to me, I was creating the opportunity for me to be so much happier!

Why are we taught so many things the wrong way round? How much time and energy do we waste beating ourselves up for the things that we'd be happy to smile at indulgently in others?

ARE YOU WEARING A MASK?

To be fair, getting to the point where you like yourself isn't quite as easy as it sounds. We know every dark and dastardly deed we've ever committed as well as those we wished we'd committed! Perceiving ourselves to be the hosts of such negativity, we tend to believe that we are indeed miserable sinners – a truth that we try to hide. Many of us are wearing masks – hoping that others will take us at face value and not delve into the squidgy parts of ourselves that we studiously try to avoid. But it's this kind of thinking that gets us into trouble. When we believe that we have to hide our true selves, we're manipulating both ourselves and other people. Without knowing quite why, other people sense that we're being inauthentic which makes them feel uneasy in our company – hardly a good foundation for healthy relationships. Worse, we use up so much energy on creating our personal 'spin' that we have little resource left for actively manifesting our dreams.

From this perspective, it's easy to see how people sabotage themselves and worse, how they keep themselves small. This happened to Alana, a client of mine who for years had been deeply unhappy and who admitted that she had a deep-seated fear of being 'found out'. Fear of not being good enough drives many of us to work harder and harder in a bid to quell the gnawing anxiety that we're going to be unmasked. Many stories involving workaholics are similar to Alana's – and very often the cause of this form of perfectionism stems back to childhood …

Alana was the youngest of three children – and being nearly ten years younger than her youngest sibling, she'd grown used to being labelled a 'mistake'. Telling me she was sure that her parents had loved her, Alana at first dismissed the notion that being called a 'mistake' may have given her a skewed view of herself.

> **Guru Success Tip**
>
> Don't wear a mask to cover up the fact that you don't think you're 'good enough'. Other people can 'feel' through the mask, and because they know intuitively that you're being inauthentic, they'll find it hard to trust you.

Alana confessed that at work, she believed everyone else knew more than she did. She was constantly stressed as she felt she had to prove herself continuously. With a wry smile, she said, 'I feel as though I have to prove myself in order to justify my presence. It's as though I feel that *I have to earn* my place on the senior management team.'

Recognising that she was getting close to the source of her deep-seated anxiety, Alana was eager to explore further – wanting to heal her feelings of inadequacy once and for all.

I asked her to close her eyes, and directed her – in her imagination – to go back to the first time that she'd felt inadequate and powerless. Slipping easily into the exercise, Alana first remembered a time when her brother had threatened her with violence if she told her parents what he'd been up to with his friends.

'OK, forgive him and let the memory fade', I said gently. 'Now travel back to the time when you first felt powerless.' Alana's face began to crumple and tears welled at the corner of her eyes.

'It's my first day at school', she said in a childish voice, 'and I don't want to be here. There's so much noise and everyone is laughing and it looks as though everyone has made friends but I'm standing in the corner on my own. I'm very lonely and frightened. I'm asking Mummy to take me home, but she's shaking her head and she's going to leave me here. I don't want to be here, I want to go home with Mummy.'

Alana nodded when I asked her if she felt abandoned. Gently, I moved her on in time and Alana admitted that although she still felt frightened she learned that if she was 'good', the teachers would be nice to her … and if she did everything her friends wanted, then they would be nice to her too. The seeds were sown. Alana had learned that in order to survive she needed to be 'good' – and that putting others first kept her safe. It was at this point that she started to lose her identity and learned how to be the person that others wanted her to be. Awareness of the root cause of her problems was the key to her healing – but in order for her to move on, the adult Alana needed to reconnect with her childhood self. I asked Alana (still as her child-self) to imagine she was standing in front of a long mirror.

'Now', I directed, 'look in the mirror and you will see the grown-up version of you.' Alana did so – telling the adult version that she needed her help and protection.

'Invite the grown-up to step out of the mirror', I continued, 'and give her a big hug!' Tears streamed down Alana's cheeks and I asked her to imagine that both parts of herself were merging to become one. I finished off the session and brought Alana back to waking reality.

> **Guru Success Tip**
>
> Remember that whatever you think about yourself, your reputation is only alive in other people's minds!

'That's incredible', she said, smiling and crying at the same time. 'It's strange, I feel like a grown-up at last!'

As Alana discovered, it's only when we're able to leave the past behind that we can get on with creating our future, as powerful grown-ups. And one of the delightful by-products of leaving the past behind us is that we're able to begin learning to love ourselves. Not in a 'hearts and flowers' way – but with a profound sense of acceptance, appreciation and gratitude.

Without self-acceptance, we invite self-loathing. Without self-appreciation, we invite self-recrimination and without self-gratitude we invite self-discontent. And all of these things breed further negativity as we start to treat ourselves harshly and without love. Think about it for a moment, do you honestly want what's best for someone you really don't like? If you don't like yourself, how well are you going to treat yourself? And yet you're the one person with whom you're going to spend your entire life!

Why *do* people dislike themselves? While there may be many reasons, often held since childhood, most can ultimately be distilled down to:

- Fear

- Guilt

- Anger

- Rejection

FEAR

There are two types of fear. The first is reality-based and is built on experience. This type of fear is healthy. Feeling fear, we don't run off the edge of the cliff screaming to the winds, 'I can fly, I can fly!' Fear ensures our physical survival. The negative experiences we go through teach us what to avoid in the future. But so far we've only been talking about the type of experiences that are based in cold, hard reality. What about those experiences that are based purely on our personal perceptions? This is the second kind of fear – the fear that resides solely in our imaginations. It's our beliefs – and to some extent our values – that often cause us to be fearful. Dealing with reality – however awful – is somehow much easier than dealing with what our imaginations manage to conjure up for us. Our fantasies (especially the negative ones) are far more powerful than reality – ask anyone who's awoken in the middle of the night worrying! The subconscious mind doesn't distinguish between vivid imagination and reality. Our emotional fears don't serve us – how can they, they're not based in truth. They only keep us small. Fear is born from the ego and, as you'll soon be discovering, the ego is the greatest illusion of all!

Our minds are constructed in such a way that when we experience an event we store the memory permanently – *along with the emotions we felt at the time.* These emotions go on to colour our perceptions, which is why our fearful fantasies can be so powerful.

GUILT

Guilt takes many guises – but of all our feelings, it is the most useless of all. The only purpose guilt serves is to teach us that we don't feel good when we do something we perceive as 'wrong'. By feeling bad, we learn not to repeat the behaviour. Once we've learned the lesson, we no longer *need* the feeling of guilt. But most of us don't drop the feelings – instead we add them to our ever-growing pile of perceived (and feared) 'wickedness', which means that as time goes on we feel worse and worse about ourselves. We've already seen the damage that self-loathing can do and by holding on to guilt we just make things even worse.

What's particularly interesting about guilt is that we often end up addicted to the behaviours that made us feel guilty in the first place. Why? Once again, it's due to the powers of the sub-conscious mind, which tends to think in images – and works hard to deliver whatever it is that we spend our time thinking about. If, to give you a very superficial example, you spend your time thinking about how bad you feel for eating a chocolate bar when you'd promised yourself not to break your diet this week, then the chances are that you'll start to fixate on the thought of a chocolate bar. Unfortunately, your subconscious mind doesn't distinguish between what's good and what's bad for you – it just thinks that if you're thinking about it, then its job is to bring it into your reality. And before you know it, as if in a trance, you find yourself raiding the chocolate cupboard! The only way to avoid self-defeating behaviour is to keep in mind what you *want* (a slim body in our example) rather than what you don't want! As the old adage goes, 'Be careful what you wish for'! We'll be investigating the power of the sub-conscious mind – and how you can use it to harness your co-creating abilities – in more depth shortly …

> **Guru Success Tip**
>
> We give ourselves far harsher 'sentences' for our 'crimes' than any court in the land would ever hand out! Lighten up and show yourself some compassion!

Guilt causes untold misery. Take a moment and think about the things that you have done which make you feel guilty. Have you learned the lessons from the guilt and moved on, or are you still behaving in the same way and still feeling guilty? To get out of the vicious cycle you have a choice: either drop the activity or drop the guilt …

Contrary to popular belief, other people cannot make you feel guilty. They can, however, shine a light on areas in which you feel vulnerable. If you stop to think about it, all of our relationships are in our heads – and even in our hearts – so any manipulation takes place there too! Because 'I' is so important to us, we have a lot invested in making sure that 'I' is always seen in the best possible light. It stands to reason therefore, that the more we are run by our self-important 'I', the more we are open to being manipulated in one guise or another by other people. But there's the rub. We think that other people are doing it to us but in reality, we're doing it to ourselves.

ANGER

Anger, as some wag once said, is just one letter short of *danger*. There's nothing wrong with anger – it's just a feeling. Stub your toe or have a run-in with a traffic warden and the chances are, you'll feel some anger. Just how much depends on your natural disposition. However, anger can become dangerous – when you hang on to it for more time than is appropriate. If you find yourself talking to anyone who'll listen about something that made you angry for days – or even weeks, months or years – after the event, then the chances are that you're hanging on to anger inappropriately.

At best, holding on to anger in this way will turn you into a victim – at worst, the resulting bitterness will start to affect your physical body. Arthritis is believed to be far more prevalent among individuals who turn their anger inwards on to themselves – and heart disease is more common among angry individuals, as my friend Ian was to discover.

Ian, a photographer, was in his mid-40s when he had his first heart attack. Half English and half Italian, Ian was famous for his 'Latin' temperament. While he was great to have at parties – his stories always had everyone doubled up with laughter – when he was on his own, he would lapse into his darker side.

Throughout his life, Ian had lived on a short fuse and was quick to lose his temper with anyone who got in his way. Road rage was an everyday occurrence for Ian who had perfected a special language of hand signals to express his fury at other road users! While he did manage to keep his cool with his clients, his associates on the other hand were so used to his regular outbursts that they no longer took any notice of

> **Guru Success Tip**
>
> While there's nothing wrong with feeling angry when it's appropriate, hanging on to the emotion long after the event has passed turns you into a victim!

him. Several privately thought that it was about time he 'grew up' but perhaps unsurprisingly, no one volunteered to tell him.

I first met Ian when he came for a hypnotherapy session to give up smoking. His doctors had warned him that another heart attack could be fatal. As it was, he'd already had surgery and his health was of serious concern to everyone. The problem was that Ian had absolutely no desire to give up smoking. He liked using a cigarette as a 'punctuation mark' in the day – an opportunity to unwind after completing a particular task.

In my experience, smokers often use cigarettes to create a 'smokescreen' around themselves – attempting to avoid an issue they don't want to look at. Ian was no exception. He'd been angry for years. Angry at his parents for not giving him the financial support he'd needed when he first started up in business; angry at his wife for refusing to be a stay-at-home wife and insisting that she wanted to pursue her own career; and angry at his colleagues for not working as hard as he did.

As we talked, Ian could see that while the smoking obviously didn't help, it was his anger that was at the root of his health problems. As he started telling me about how the nurses had treated him so badly in hospital – and about their rudeness – he relived the experience all over again. It wasn't just that he was repeating the story – he was reliving it, as evidenced by his red face and the bulging veins in his neck. Worse, he was reliving the whole experience every time he could find someone to listen to his litany of woes. If Ian was to avoid death, it was critical that we found him a way to deal with his anger.

Ian thought that he was good at handling his anger as he didn't bottle up his feelings in any way.

'Yes, you're right', I said, 'bottling up your feelings wouldn't be the answer. But nor is your current way of coping. Can you see that by reliving your angry experiences in your mind, you're putting yourself in a heightened fight-or-flight state, which is putting severe pressure on your body?'

'Hmmm', he replied.

'As the saying goes, if you don't like the results you're getting, then change what you're doing! Let's work out a strategy for you to *deal* with your anger rather than just express it.'

'Yup, that kinda makes sense', he said half smiling, 'so, come on then – how do I deal with my anger?'

I went on to explain to Ian that there are five stages to dealing with negativity and these are: Expression, Forgiveness, Acceptance, Love and Letting Go. I gently took Ian through these five stages with regard to all the relationships and events that had made him angry. Having used the process, he was confident that he'd be able to use the tools on his own. By the end of the session he admitted that he was exhausted. Ian came to see me again a month later to report on his progress. 'Everyone's noticed how much calmer I am, so thank you. My wife thinks you must be something of a miracle worker!'

'Not at all', I said, 'You're the one doing the miracles – I'm just the signpost.'

Frustratingly, Ian never did manage to quit smoking, although he cut down substantially. He is, however, in much better health and his heart problems have, to date, stabilised.

Ian's story is an extreme example of a common theme. You'll learn more about the process for dealing with negative emotions shortly.

REJECTION

Finally, we come to one of our greatest fears of all: the fear of rejection. It's human nature to feel the need to be part of the tribe, not least because safety in numbers increases our chances of survival. However, as we begin to follow our soul's yearning for spiritual enlightenment we discover that all too often we're going to have to give up our craving for other people's approval. Living a life in which we seek approval above all else means that we keep ourselves small – fearing that if we don't subsume our needs to those of our family, friends or peers, then we'll face rejection. It's only when we're able to like – and indeed love – ourselves that we become free of other people's approval which means that we're free to make the type of decisions that empower us.

The problem with our fear of rejection is that it has a tendency to become a self-fulfilling prophecy. Remember how the subconscious mind works hard to bring the things we think about it into reality? Well, the same applies with our fear of rejection, which actually arises through low self-esteem. When we fear that we're not good enough, we not only try to cover it up, but also adapt our behaviours so that others aren't able to

> **Guru Success Tip**
>
> The more you crave other people's approval, the more likely you are to experience rejection!

see through to the 'real' us. But the problem is that we still know that the 'real' us is hidden in there somewhere, and as a consequence we start to worry that others will see through us and find out what we're really like! In my experience, this vicious cycle of low self-esteem and fear of being found out is at the heart of most perfectionism and over-work. It's only when we're truly comfortable with ourselves and accept that we're lovable simply for being who we are, rather than having to earn love, that we can let the pattern go.

Often there's a cost in life. Many high achievers suffer from the patterns I've just described but instead of living life as a victim, they've used their fear to fuel ever increasing levels of success. Outsiders view these people as 'hardworking' at best and 'lucky' at worst, not realising that their drive and ambition comes from the fear of the humiliation of being unmasked rather than from a passion for success. High achievers who are driven by fear are seldom at peace. For them, achievements tend to feel both fleeting and empty.

Paradoxically, fear can be a great motivational tool – in the same way that a grain of sand enables a pearl to form in an oyster. But with the pearl, we appreciate its beauty – and we need to learn to do the same with our successes. How often do you stop to celebrate? Does achieve-ment feel like victory – or does it feel hollow, and do you find yourself immediately turning to the next goal in the hope that perhaps this will fill the empty gap inside?

Interestingly, the emptiness that we seek to fill through achievement is due to the lack of love that we have for ourselves. In our imaginations, we greatly fear rejection from others – but in reality it is we who reject ourselves! The only way in the long term to overcome emptiness and low self-esteem is to work on creating a great relationship with your-self. Treat yourself as someone you truly care about! How do you treat someone you love? What do you do for them to make them happy? Think about how you listen to what's important to them and how you encourage, inspire and motivate them. Consider also how you're prepared to forgive them their faults and love them unconditionally. Think how good life would be if you decided to treat yourself in the same way!

Chapter 5
Pete turns stress to his advantage

*N*ext into the boardroom was Pete. Dressed in a tweed jacket, checked shirt and sharply pressed black trousers, he was the eldest of the trio I was due to see that day. Revered within the bank for his knowledge and experience, Pete's air of professionalism seemed to be covering something that felt almost like resignation. It didn't take me too long to discover why.

Once Pete had completed his wheel of life, it became clear that it was his career that was causing him the most concern. Most of his scores were around 7 – but he had marked his career at only 3. Surprised, I asked him the reason for the low score.

'I'm tired', he replied. 'Every year I hit the targets they give me – but instead of being satisfied, they just give me a steeper target the following year. It used to be fun but now it's just a grind. And when I look into the future, I can only see it getting worse, not better!'

Surprised at Pete's candour, I asked him to outline his personal goals for me.

'Just surviving is all I'm focused on. To be honest, I've not been sleeping very well and my wife has noticed that I've not been myself either. I've been getting very snappy with her and recently we've had quite a few rows. I'm sorry, I didn't mean to moan – what are we meant to be doing in this session?'

'I don't think you're moaning at all – and that's exactly what this session is for, after all! Tell me about your targets – did you have a hand in setting them?'

'Well, that's a moot point', Pete had laughed. 'Originally, we set the targets at the level we thought we could achieve and then we gave these figures to our line managers, who in turn passed them up the chain for approval. But by the time the figures came all the way back down to us, they'd been revised upwards so much that they were barely recognisable. The trouble is the same thing happened last year – and the year before, come to that, and everyone in the team pulled out all the stops to achieve the impossible. It would seem that the "powers that be" believe we can do the same thing again this year but to be honest, I just don't have the stomach for it any more.'

Pete's was a common story and I knew all too well that if we didn't sort out the situation pretty quickly he was in danger of completely burning out. Being signed off long term for stress held no appeal for Pete and I knew that his bosses wouldn't have been pleased either. It was time to reframe the situation.

*'Pete', I asked, 'I'm serious this time, what really are your **personal** goals?'*

'I don't know that I have any. I suppose like most people I want to be happy and healthy and know that my family are too. There's nothing that I really need.'

Knowing that goals create personal motivation and an energy of their own, I wasn't prepared to drop the matter there. Gently I pressed him again, 'If I could give you a magic wand and you could have anything you wanted – anything at all – what would you wish for?'

At first Pete just kept staring down at the table. Then I noticed a flicker of something bordering on excitement cross his face – but in an instant it was gone.

'You just thought of something! Go on – tell me what it was …'

'Well …'

'It's OK, I won't make you stick to it … but at least tell me!'

'Well, I've always thought that it would be lovely to be able to retire to a nice house in France but frankly, there's no way we'd be able to afford it.'

'OK, I know you can't afford it, but let's amuse ourselves for a moment and see if we can find a way in which you could afford it.'

Pete looked at me as though I was mad. Used to being on the receiving end of 'that look', and being confident in where we were going with the discussion, I chose to focus solely on the matter in hand. In his early 50s, Pete probably had at least a decade to go until his retirement, so I knew that we had some time on our side if we were going to work out a plan to make his dream come true.

Together we worked how much extra – in commission – Pete would earn if he managed to hit the new targets that he'd been given for the year. I then asked Pete if he would be prepared to invest that extra commission in a ten year savings plan. He'd nodded.

'OK' I said, 'you know that I'm not a maths wizard – but how much do you think you'd be likely to have accrued in ten years time?'

The silence was heavy in the room. Pete was clearly working things out in his head. After a few moments, it was as though a light had been switched on in his eyes. Excitedly, he said, 'Do you know, with properties being so much cheaper in France, I think that if I started saving now in the way that you're suggesting, I could actually make that retirement home a reality!'

Wanting to keep him in that state of excited possibility, I asked Pete to imagine what it would be like to live in the kind of property that he and his wife wanted. More animated than I'd ever seen him, he started talking about a stone house with cream window frames and a beautiful cottage garden with a riot of vividly coloured flowers.

I then asked him how it would feel sitting in the bright and sunny garden, knowing that it was through his efforts that he'd managed to make his and his wife's dream come true.

'Ah, it's just wonderful. I feel so free, and the sensation of the sun on my face is delightful.'

'Great, you're looking around you and really enjoying the fruits of your labours. Now, I want you to imagine that you think back to this time today and know that it was the decision you made in this session today that made your dream home possible. How do you feel now?'

Contemplating life as though he was living ten years in the future in his French cottage, Pete smiled and said, 'It's curious but as I look back to when I made the decision to follow my heart, it was as though I had a sense of control again in my life. I really enjoyed work in those last ten years – it felt as though I was working for "me" and to be honest, it was exciting!'

'Eh voila!' I laughed, bringing him back to the present. 'How do you feel now?' I hardly needed to ask. Pete had more colour in his cheeks and the gleam was still there in his eyes.

The next task in hand was for Pete to start preparing an action plan. That was his homework for our next session together. But for now, this session was drawing to a close.

'OK, Pete. You've got your homework, which is to work out how you're going to hit your targets. You'll be working out what you can do differently to make better use of your time – and also be thinking about who else can help you reach your objectives. But, what's the one thing you can do today that will show your subconscious mind that you're serious about this new commitment?'

Gathering up his papers and shoving them all untidily into his well-worn briefcase, he replied, 'Oh, that's easy. I'm off right now to start a new savings plan in my name – and I'll be investing the commission I earn on it too, to give the whole enterprise a kick start!'

With that Pete shook my hand slightly longer than was necessary – but with a real warmth that suggested that he was now more hopeful about the future than he'd felt for a long while.

Points to ponder as you start to …
Be your own guru

1 How would you like to see your life in ten years' time? Five years' time? One year's time?

2 What would you need to do to achieve these goals?

3 What kind of limiting behaviours would you need to give up?

4 How can you use the work you do now to create your future? Can you use some of what you earn to help you become better qualified? Does your current job give you time to study or pursue the kind of hobby that you could later turn into a paying career? What advice would you give someone in your situation?

5 Who are you blaming and what excuses are you using for remaining 'stuck' where you are?

6 How would it feel to have created the level of success that you only dream of today? How would your life look? Imagine that this 'scene' is in the middle of a film about your life. What did the person playing you in the movie do in order to achieve that success? What can you do, starting today, to turn the vision into a reality?

Chapter 6
Getting to the real cause of stress

We tend to say that we feel stressed when we feel out of control – or are overwhelmed by a situation. This kind of stress is actually more accurately labelled 'distress' and if it's allowed to go on for any length of time, it will have an increasingly negative effect on both our body and psyche. There is, however, another kind of stress – called 'eustress' which is the kind of feeling we have when we feel highly motivated to do something or when we're pushing ourselves out of our comfort zone. Indeed, it's said that we need a certain amount of eustress in our lives, for without it we'd simply become couch potatoes!

The effect of both types of stress tend to be the same on our bodies – increased heart rate and more rapid breathing being two examples. However eustress is only felt for short bursts of time, while distress tends to be more long term – and it's long term stress that causes physical and emotional damage.

Often, by reframing a situation we can change a feeling of distress into one of eustress – especially when we're able to create a sense of purpose. Usually we believe that the cause of our stress is external, blaming events or other people. But when it comes down to it, all of our stress is in our heads! It's not the events or other people that are having the damaging effect on us – rather, it's how we choose to perceive and respond to those outside events and people that causes our physical and mental reactions. When we understand this, we're able to put ourselves at 'cause' rather than 'effect'. Do you give your power away by blaming other people and circumstances?

> **Guru Success Tip**
>
> When we can align our goals with those of our employer, there's no room for stress because everyone's on to a winner!

DEALING WITH STRESSFUL SITUATIONS AT WORK …

Until we have a clear personal reason 'why' we are working, we feel that we're cannon fodder in the relentless war to increase profits. The result is burn-out and depleted energy levels. But when we work to fulfil our own purpose, we're excited, creative and full of energy. When you align your goals with those of your employer, there's no room for stress because everyone is on to a winner!

Little was I to know – but during my initial one-to-one sessions with my pilot group of nine at the bank, I would go on to 'sell' three managers their own savings plans. Using their jobs in this way to seed fund their aspirations created a level of sustained motivation – not least because, at last, the people involved had managed to find an answer to that most important of questions: 'What's in it for me?'!

Once we have a clear idea of our own personal goals, managing time becomes a lot easier too. Every decision is simply benchmarked against whether or not it enhances our ability to attain our dream, as my self-employed client Rob was to find out …

When I first met Rob, he'd looked tired and depressed – admitting that running his own catering business had not been as much fun as he'd anticipated. Close to burn-out and anxious about the future, he'd finally decided that enough was enough. As his story unfolded, Rob told me that he had he hadn't taken any holiday over the preceding 18 months – and even over the Christmas holiday he had ended up in bed with flu rather than enjoying his time off. Recognising that he couldn't sustain his workaholic lifestyle had prompted Rob to book a session with me to see how he could alleviate his stress.

I first suggested that we look at how Rob was managing his time. Looking at his feet, he replied that he never had the chance to manage his time because all of his days were spent dealing with problems as they arose. His only was to keep the company afloat – he had no aspirations beyond that.

Already it was clear that this was where the root of Rob's problems lay. By crisis managing all the time, Rob had no spare capacity for planning – and yet it was this lack of planning that was causing Rob to be in a permanent state of crisis in the first place. His was also something of a joyless existence which was also contributing to his feeling drained. It was a double-bind situation that many people running their own businesses find themselves facing sooner or later.

Guru Success Tip

A lack of planning will leave you working in a permanent state of crisis management!

I outlined to Rob that one of the secrets of good time management was to focus and prioritise – with the ultimate aim of spending all work time on matters that were important but not yet urgent. 'At the moment, all your time is spent on activities that are both important and urgent', I said, 'and this is what is causing your stress levels to rise.'

Shaking his head in protest, Rob said, 'I understand what you're saying – but to be honest, I think I'm at my best when I'm under stress. If I don't have deadlines looming or clients demanding attention, I tend to switch off.' Rob went on to admit that he tended to multitask, which gave him a buzz – and made him feel in control and dynamic.

'I can see how it might feel that way', I told Rob, 'but actually, however good you may feel, your body is still reacting to stress signals. Not only does stress have a negative effect on the body – making the immune system less effective, as you found out at Christmas – but it also has a major impact on your creative abilities.' Rob had frowned – and then asked me to explain. 'Well', I said, 'when your body is under stress, the "flight or fight" response is induced. Our bodies are unable to calibrate the level of threat to our being, it's as though there is simply an on/off switch. Or in other words, our response to threats will always be identical, whether we are face-to-face with a sabre-toothed tiger or whether we are face-to-face with a towering in-tray.

'When we're responding to a threat, our bodies start to function in survival mode – which means that our more sophisticated bodily functions cease to work properly. Digestion, for example, is not necessary to our immediate survival, so when we find ourselves in a stressful situation, blood and oxygen are immediately diverted to our muscles and to the primitive part of our brain only (the amygdala) that deals with "fight or flight".

'Because the more sophisticated parts of the brain are not receiving optimum amounts of blood and oxygen, our ability to listen to anything rational or "see the logic" in an explanation is dramatically diminished. Similarly, creativity is not necessary for the "fight or flight" response and therefore our abilities to innovate – let alone problem solve – are impaired.'

Having understood the reasons why he needed to change his way of approaching work, Rob and I spent the rest of our time together looking at what he wanted to achieve personally through having his own business – and then created a work schedule that would enable him to catch up with the backlog and plan properly for the future.

Chapter 7
Matt discovers the childhood reason for his shaking hands

*M*att looked across the table at me, wondering just what this session was going to be about. The only advice he'd been given was to keep an open mind. Judging by the cynical look on his face, his mind was anything but. A bright young man with, by all accounts, a glittering future ahead of him, there was something cold about him.

I gave Matt a wheel of life to complete and he gave himself an 8 for each topic. He filled the wheel in too quickly to have given it much thought and it was becoming clearer by the moment that he had no intention of opening up to me. I'd met people like Matt before and I was determined that his aloofness wasn't going to faze me.

I asked him about his career and he told me that he'd always wanted to follow his father into banking. 'He made a great success of his career and earned lots of money – and I want to do the same', he said.

'So do you have any long term goals?' I asked.

'Of course', he replied, not giving anything away.

'That's great – are they SMART goals?'

'It depends on what you mean by "smart." Do you mean smart as in well thought out and planned?'

'In a way', I replied. 'SMART stands for "Specific," "Measurable," "Achievable," "Ritten" and "Timed." Some people say that the "R" stands for realistic but I think "realistic" and "achievable" are pretty much the same things. And writing something down conveys a commitment to your subconscious mind that you're serious! Whenever you sign your name, for example, you're making a commitment and doubtless you had it drummed into you as a child that you must read the small print before you sign a document!'

Matt nodded and gave me a half smile. 'You mentioned the subconscious mind – that's something I'd be interested in learning more about.'

'That's good – because we'll be looking at the subconscious mind and the power it has over us when we all get together for our two days' training. A lot of what we'll be covering will be experiential rather than theoretical, so I think you'll really enjoy it.'

Already Matt had begun to perk up. It was as though he was thinking that this wasn't going to be the traditional type of training he'd expected.

Refusing to be sidetracked, I brought Matt back to the subject of goals and aspirations. 'Having a sense of personal purpose gives you energy and drive – goals are like signposts that help keep you on your path. Knowing where you're headed is the key to success but surprisingly few people have any idea of their personal purpose, let alone their goals. If you don't know where you're going, it's going to be pretty hard to get there. Goals on their own aren't enough. They're just a part of the jigsaw puzzle that will go on to make up the picture of your life. To be effective, goals need to be backed up with an action plan of how they'll be achieved. A goal without an action plan is little more than wishful thinking. Goals not only help you to remain *consciously focused but they also give the subconscious mind something to sink its teeth into.'*

Matt was leaning forward slightly now – a sure sign that he was becoming more and more interested in what I had to say. 'Tell me about the power of SMART goals', he asked.

I started to describe how to be powerful, goals must first be 'Specific'. 'For example, saying "I want to earn more money" is just wishful thinking. But putting a figure on "more money" like say, "£50,000 a year" makes it clear.'

'It's also important to be able to monitor your progress in attaining a goal – and to be able to assess when you've accomplished it, which is why it must be "Measurable."'

Seeing Matt's slight frown, I gave another example. 'If you decide that you really want to own a little red sports car, you can measure your success by looking out at your driveway. When that car's parked outside, you know your mission is accomplished!'

I then went on to explain to Matt that goals have to be 'Achievable'. 'I can wish all I like to be a famous Harlem Globetrotter, but we both know that I'll never be male or tall enough – let alone fit enough', I laughed.

'I've already explained why goals should be written down – so all we're left with now is the "T" of SMART, which stands for "Timed." If you don't set yourself a completion time for your goal, then the chances of you achieving it are horribly diminished. Knowing when you want to achieve your goal is essential for creating a practical action plan. For example, if you wanted to lose two stone in weight, your approach would be dictated by whether you wanted to lose the weight over three months or three years! In order to achieve the weight loss in three months, you'd have to go on a stringent diet and vigorous exercise programme, whereas if you allowed yourself three years to lose the weight, you could probably get away with some minor but long term changes. Do you see what I'm getting at?'

Matt gave me a thumbs up, so I continued.

'Of course, not all of our goals need to be materialistic, in fact I'd suggest that they probably shouldn't be – but describing the principles using tangible examples just makes it easier.

'And in order to make your goals more realistic, it really helps to visualise them strongly. Imagine what it would be like to have accomplished your dream. What would it look like? How would it feel? The more strongly you can connect with your senses in this regard, the more powerful the message is to your subconscious mind. But I'm getting ahead of myself. We'll be talking a lot more on the course about how the subconscious mind processes thoughts – and I know that you'll find it fascinating – but for now you're going to have to make do with understanding the power of SMART goals!'

Matt had smiled at this and as he picked up his mug to take a drink, I noticed that his hand had a very slight tremor, sending ripples through the milky coffee. I asked him why his hand shook.

He replied that his hand had always shaken since he was a child and that it was a source of great amusement to his family.

'Would you like to find out why?'

'Sure', *said Matt who, like me, had no idea what was about to unfold.*

'OK, let's try a fun exercise, using your subconscious mind. In a moment, we're going to be "having a conversation" with your hand to see what message it can give us.'

With that, Matt rolled his eyes and I could see his scepticism rising once again.

'Bear with me, what we're about to do may seem strange to your rational left brain, but your creative right brain will enjoy the ride, I promise.'

I invited Matt to close his eyes and begin to imagine a tiny version of himself that could move around his body at will in order to investigate any problems. Having ascertained that Matt could indeed see his tiny 'alter ego', I asked 'Little Matt' if it was safe for him to investigate the source of the shaking hand. Matt nodded. I then told Matt that all he needed to do at this stage was to act as an interpreter between Little Matt and myself, relaying my questions and his answers.

'OK, Little Matt, please travel all the way down into Matt's hand and tell us what you see.'

At first, there was no audible response. But I could see that the blood was beginning to drain from Matt's face, making him very pale.

'It's OK, Little Matt. You're completely safe and secure. You're here to help Matt understand the cause of his shaking hand. You know that his tremor is a symptom and not a cause and today, with your help, we're going to reach the cause. Tell me what you see.'

His voice was hoarse, barely a whisper. 'That's strange, I can see my old music teacher', said Matt. A tear started to form in his right eye and after several minutes, he punctuated the silence saying, 'You shouldn't be doing that to me.' Clearly Matt was now talking directly with his music teacher.

'Go on Matt, tell me what you see. What is your music teacher doing?'

'He's touching me. He shouldn't be touching me there. It's not right. I'm frightened. He's hurting me.'

At that Matt broke down and started to sob.

Allowing him to shed the tears that had obviously been repressed for so long – locked away with the memories of what had happened to him when he was a little boy – I simply kept quiet, passing him a tissue occasionally from the box I always brought with me for just such eventualities.

As the sobs began to subside, I suggested that together we could bring some healing to the situation. Taking him through a similar process to the one experienced by Jenny earlier in the day, I said, 'Matt, in your imagination, I want you to look your old music teacher in the eye and invite him to sit down, while you continue to stand. That way you'll be bigger than him and already you feel more powerful, don't you?'

Matt nodded.

'Good, now first of all, I want you to tell your music teacher how much he frightened you and how angry you are that he behaved in that way towards you. Tell him out loud – and tell him to his face.'

Matt began speaking, hesitantly at first but his words quickly gathered pace as he got into his stride. 'I hate you for what you did to me. I knew what you were doing wasn't right and I felt so ashamed. I didn't dare tell anyone because you threatened me, saying that no one would believe me.'

Carrying on in the same vein for a little while, there came a point when Matt had got all the humiliation, hurt and anger out of his system. He took a deep breath and let out a deep sigh. I knew that he was ready to go on to the next stage in the process.

'OK Matt, you're doing really well', I reassured him. 'Now, I want you to listen carefully to my words. I'm sure that you'd agree that you no longer want this man to have any power over you. The way to set yourself free is to forgive him – not because you condone his actions but because all the time you're angry with him, there's still an energetic connection between you both. Does this make sense to you?'

'I don't want to forgive him.'

'I know you don't and he had no right to do what he did to you. But let's look at it this way. All the time you're carrying this around with you – even subconsciously – you're the one being affected by what happened to you. Your music teacher doesn't know how you feel – for all you know, he could

be dead by now. When you think about it, he's not being affected by your anger – only you are. Don't you think it's time to set yourself free? After all, you're forgiving for your sake – not for his. And the less you feel like forgiving him, the more you need to. I know it's hard, but I guarantee that you'll feel better.'

I went on to explain that the subconscious mind holds on to all the memories of everything that's ever happened to us, along with the emotions we felt at the time of the event. While we can't change the events from the past, we can change how we feel about them now.

'Let's start with something that you can perhaps forgive the teacher for …'

After a long pause, Matt said, 'OK', very softly. Taking a deep breath, he said, 'I suppose I can forgive him for making me feel that I'd asked for it and for threatening me.'

'Good, now tell him that. Look him in the eye, in your imagination, and tell him that.'

'Mr Brown, I choose to forgive you for making me feel that it was my fault. I forgive you for humiliating me and I forgive you for frightening me. But I can't forgive you for what you did to me, I just can't.'

*Putting my hand on his shoulder, I told Matt that I knew it was hard – but that forgiving Mr Brown for **everything** was necessary if he, Matt, was going to be free of the effects of the past.*

'The thing to remember is that our bodies tend to express what's going on in our minds, it's as though our body is a messenger, telling us what needs to be healed in our minds. If we ignore the messages, then we tend to find that our bodies create a stronger form of dis-ease. Your hand tremor is just a symptom and you've already done all the work to find out the cause. Dealing with the symptoms is never enough, for a long lasting healing to take place you have to deal with the cause. Now that you know this, you know it makes sense to forgive Mr Brown, don't you?'

With an almost imperceptible nod of the head, Matt cleared his throat, eventually saying, 'Mr Brown … I forgive you … I choose to forgive you … I forgive you for what you did to me … all of it.'

I passed Matt another tissue as more tears began to roll down his cheeks.

'Great work, well done! Now, I want you to make the decision to accept Mr Brown as he is. Of course, I'm not saying that his behaviour was in any way acceptable but it's only when you acknowledge him for who and what he is that you'll be able to move on. And the all-important thing is that you've moved on …'

'Mr Brown', said Matt in a slightly resigned voice, 'I accept you for who you are but I'll never condone what you did to me. But', he added in a stronger tone, 'Today I've changed. You've no longer got any power over me.'

'Excellent. Now it's time for you to invite him to leave. Thank him for being here to talk with you today and tell him that it's time for him to go. Watch as he walks towards the door and, as he puts his hand on the door handle he turns round to look at you one last time. Tell him that it really is time for him to go – and that he goes with your blessing.'

Listening to Matt finish the process, I knew that he'd sleep well that night. I invited him to open his eyes, which he did – blinking several times as he grew accustomed to the bright sunshine which was now streaming through the boardroom window. Neither of us spoke for what seemed like a minute. Eventually Matt broke the silence, saying that before today, he'd had no memories of Mr Brown.

'That was really weird. It's only now that I realise just how far "out of it" I felt when we did that exercise.' *Shaking his head in disbelief, he admitted that in a strange way he felt lighter. Leaving Matt to gather his thoughts together, I left the room to make us both a cup of tea. Returning five minutes later with the great British panacea to all ills, I handed him his mug. As he picked it up, he smiled, took a sip and then carefully placed it back on the table.*

'That was pretty powerful stuff.' As he picked up his drink again, he exclaimed with laughter in his voice, 'Do you know – this is the first time in years that I haven't seen concentric circles in my mug! If I'm honest, I'd thought all this training and stuff was going to be pretty much a waste of time, but it seems that I was mistaken. Sorry.'

'Nothing to forgive', I said. 'And I promise you, the fun's only just begun!'

Matt smiled, a genuine warm smile that crinkled the sides of his eyes, and said, 'If I'm really honest, I've always found this psychological stuff really interesting but whenever I've tried talking about it with anyone else, they just accuse me of being weird! How can I find out more about what we did? Can I use the process on myself, or can I only go through it with you? Will we be doing more of this stuff on the course?'

It seemed as though I had touched on something within Matt and we both somehow felt a growing bond. 'You bet we'll be doing a lot more of this kind of stuff on the course. Not only will get to understand the power of your subconscious mind, but you'll also be learning about your mind/body connection. And as if that's not enough, you'll also be discovering how to create really effective relationships – all based on this "psychological stuff" as you put it!'

And at that, Matt had simply given me another thumbs up and a big grin.

Points to ponder as you start to ...
Be your own guru

1 Review your goals from the previous chapter and make sure that they are SMART (Specific, Measurable, Achievable, Ritten & Timed). Recognise that any goals you have that aren't SMART are just wishful thinking!

2 Start to tune into your body. You'll discover how to interpret the messages from your physical self later, but for now, simply become aware of any aches and pains that you have and where-abouts in your body they're located.

3 Make a list of the people who encouraged you and made you feel good about yourself when you were a child. How many of their attributes, attitudes and behaviours have you unwittingly adopted as an adult?

4 Make a list of the people who discouraged you and made you feel bad about yourself when you were a child. How many of their attributes, attitudes and behaviours have you unwittingly adopted as an adult?

5 How much anger, hurt or resentment – caused by other people – are you harbouring? How much happier do you think you could be if you simply chose to forgive and let go?

6 Make a list of all the people who've ever hurt you and make the decision – for your sake – to consider forgiving them. Remember that forgiving someone doesn't condone their actions but it is the key to your freedom! Keep this list, you'll need it when we get to the Personal Enlightenment and Release process.

Chapter 8
Learning to deal with negative emotions

Discovering our repressed emotions is only the first step in our healing. The most important step however, is learning how to deal with our negative feelings. Unfortunately, counsellors have an often unfair reputation for repeating the 'and how does that make you feel?' mantra to their clients. But the trick to effective self-therapy is learning how to transcend negative feelings. And most importantly, we shouldn't stir up our negative emotions for the sake of it. After all, what's to be gained by wallowing in negativity? Feeling unhappy is not our natural state – and certainly not what we were born for! So it stands to reason then, that when we feel bad, it's our internal intelligence telling us that we need to be doing something differently!

OUR NEGATIVITY HURTS ONLY US …

Remember, all the relationships we have only exist in our heads. The relationships you have with your family, for example, aren't to be found in the family home – they only exist in your and their minds! Because of this, we're able to fix any problems in our relationships in our minds too. The subconscious mind doesn't distinguish between very vivid imagination and reality, so the good news is that healing any problematic relationship in our minds is as good as doing it in reality. The benefits of this are two-fold: firstly, we don't have to go through the trauma of facing someone who may not take too kindly to our words – and who may indeed react negatively. Secondly, we can still heal a relationship even if the other person has died!

> **Guru Success Tip**
>
> All of the relationships we have exist only in our heads and hearts – which is why our heads and hearts are the best place to heal our relationships too!

A long while back, I had a client who illustrated my point perfectly. Pauline was very angry with the way she had been treated as a child and as a consequence, she hadn't experienced very much happiness as an adult …

Pauline felt that she'd been a mistake – and that if she'd been born at all, she should have been a boy. She blamed her parents for favouring her older sister and she complained of having a materially sound – but emotionally barren – childhood. As she was telling me her story, I noticed from the lines in her face that she must have been in her mid-sixties – a long time to be carrying around this unhappiness! When I suggested that perhaps it was now time to forgive her parents, she became angry – asking why she should forgive them.

'I'm not God', she said. 'No', I replied, but knowing that she was fairly religious, I added, 'but it does say in the Lord's Prayer, "forgive us our trespasses, as *we* forgive those who trespass against us."'

Suddenly, Pauline – who normally portrayed the British 'stiff upper lip' – started sobbing hysterically, shouting, 'Why should I forgive them, why should they get away with it?'

In the quiet seconds that followed, I recalled that both Pauline's parents had died in the previous six months. And I wondered just who she was hurting with her lack of forgiveness ...

UNDERSTANDING THE POWER OF EMOTION ...

So, what exactly is emotion?

Emotions are generally described as 'strong feelings' which can have a powerful effect (positive or negative) on both our mental state and physical body. Think back to a time when you felt very strongly about an event or person – how did your body feel at the time? And the converse is also true, whether our bodies are in harmony or not has an effect on how we feel psychologically.

Guru Success Tip

Remember it's your body that 'feels' – but it's your personality or ego that interprets those feelings, according to its beliefs!

It has also been said that 'emotion' equates to 'e-motion' or 'energy-in-motion'. Emotions are not the same things as our thoughts – for a start, we feel them throughout the body. We do, however, tend to rationalise our emotions with our thoughts, labelling our feelings according to our values, beliefs and past experiences. Depending on how we choose to interpret it, butterflies in the stomach can represent excitement or fear.

Our bodies do the feeling – but our personalities get to do the interpreting! Whether or not the threat is real, the emotions we experience are very real. Emotion precedes thought and, sadly, we're not able to choose our emotions. We can, however, through reframing events and deciding to let go of our attachment to our feelings, bring about swift and powerful healing. In the same way, we can't change events that actually happened in the past, but we can change how we feel about those events.

Emotions bring colour to our lives – and give us the energy to manifest what we want (or fear!) in life. The secret to successfully manifesting your dreams is first to know what you want and, second, to visualise your goals as though they have already happened – with as much positive emotion and feeling as you can muster! The continuum of human feelings ranges from love at one end to fear at the other. While we tend to grow up believing that the opposite of love is hate, the opposite of love is actually fear – with hatred being, on occasion, an outcome of fear.

Emotions ensure our survival. The sensation at the pit of our stomach when faced with the archetypal sabre-toothed tiger for example, prompts us to run for our lives. We don't have time to intellectualise in certain situations – stopping to weigh up the size, colour and ferocity of our would-be assailant would result in our untimely death! Emotions therefore help us to make split second decisions – although as we've already seen, too much negative emotion can play havoc on the body by causing it to be in a state of permanent stress/arousal.

Our subconscious mind registers every single emotion we feel and stores it within our mind, along with the memories that created the emotion. Unless we actively investigate what our subconscious mind is harbouring, we can find ourselves being driven by inappropriate emotions/memories. Often our subconscious mind is as clogged with long-out-of-date 'stuff' as the 'delete' bin on our computers!

Stored negative emotions will always go on to cause us trouble but unfortunately learning how to deal with them isn't something we were taught in school. (How different would my life have been if I'd been taught more about emotions at school – and less about the Vikings and wheat farming in North America?!)

SO JUST WHAT IS EMOTIONAL INTELLIGENCE?

Emotional intelligence is about awareness – of ourselves and our feelings and of other people and their feelings. When we're said to be 'emotionally intelligent', we're not only consciously aware of how we feel *and why* (and how other people feel and why) but we're also able to modify our behaviours to ensure we make the best of any situation for everybody – including ourselves!

When we become more emotionally aware, we begin to realise that not only can no one else control our feelings – but that we're solely responsible for our behaviours. There's a 'cause and effect' process at work with regard to our emotions: we feel first and then behave, even though the gap between the two may only be a nanosecond. The more stressed we feel, the more our reactions are driven by the primitive, reptilian part of the brain – which is responsible for the 'fight or flight' response.

Our feelings are vitally important and turning our back on them doesn't make them go away. In fact the opposite occurs, as we create a 'pressure cooker' effect – with all of our negative feelings and character traits spilling out when the stress just gets too much. In order to avoid the 'straw breaking the camel's back' syndrome, we have to deal with our feelings as and when they arise, *before* they begin to poison our internal systems.

Guru Success Tip

Remember that just because people are different, it doesn't make them wrong!

And the really great news is that it's our emotions that govern our behaviours – and that once we become consciously aware of our emotions, we're better able to choose how we behave. Or in other words, change is possible!

It's also worth bearing in mind that just because people are different – and handle their feelings and behaviours differently – it doesn't make them wrong. Ultimately, all of us have an inherent tendency towards psychological growth and well being and while there are some hardcore psychopaths about, it's likely that if you chose to read this book in the first place, you're the kind of person who wants to learn from your mistakes and move on! Perhaps the word 'compassion' is the key. All of us make mistakes – it's how we learn and grow. If you're not out there busy making mistakes, then you're probably not challenging yourself enough – which could be thought of as the greatest mistake of all!

At the end of the day, a lot of this comes down to intention. Personally, I'm far more comfortable with someone who did the wrong thing for the right reasons than someone who did the right thing for the wrong reasons!

SO WHAT ROLE DOES EMOTIONAL INTELLIGENCE HAVE TO PLAY AT WORK?

In the workplace emotional intelligence is the missing link, the glue if you like, that creates success. Successful companies employ successful individuals and emotional intelligence shortens the learning curve to profits! Research has shown that people with higher levels of emotional intelligence are better performers than their emotionally dim-witted counterparts, not least because emotional intelligence is about personal and team *effectiveness*.

Negative feelings, fairly obviously, drive our behaviours in negative ways. Knowing how to deal with them – and let them go – is therefore of paramount importance. As we've already discussed, the first step in creating a good relationship with yourself is the examination of the programmes on which your subconscious is running – and recreating them as necessary. The second step is to understand the importance of liking – even loving – yourself. Clearly, this isn't about looking in the mirror and thinking how wonderful you are, it's more about self-acceptance. Until you have self-acceptance, you'll always be operating in conflict. Do you care about the best interests of your enemies?

GET READY TO PEEL THE PEAR!

In order to be happy, healthy and wealthy we have no choice but to learn to let go of our negative feelings. Happy people don't waste time feeling angry, guilty or rejected – and they certainly don't have time to indulge in playing the 'blame game'. Every time you're unhappy, or become aware of a negative feeling in your body, you can be sure that your emotional and spiritual selves are out of kilter. When you're unbalanced in this way, you're not able to function as a 'whole' human being, which means that you've lost your integrity (having integrity is by definition about being 'entire' or 'complete'). Loss of integrity equals loss of personal power.

Our negative feelings can be aimed towards others – or turned inwards to ourselves. Popular psychology tells us that depression is anger turned inwards. Of course, we all have to learn the lessons from our mistakes, but for the sake of our health – let alone our relationships – we have to let go and move on. All the time that we're holding on to negative feelings, we're being controlled by them. Worse, there's an all too human tendency to hold on to a perceived 'slight' and repeat it over and over again in our minds. While the event happened once – or maybe more often – in the past, each time we replay it in our minds we're the ones perpetrating the abuse!

I'm not suggesting for a moment that forgiving someone who's hurt you is easy. Far from it. But until you do, your life is going to be continually affected detrimentally by someone who doesn't even have any idea how you feel! Your anger doesn't affect someone else, it only affects you! (You may feel that you're successfully punishing someone by remaining angry with them – but the punishment to yourself is far worse. Try feeling angry and happy at the same time! For that matter, try frowning and smiling at the same time. You simply can't do it!)

> **Guru Success Tip**
>
> If you're feeling self-righteous and angry, ask yourself this question: Is it better to be right or happy?

The less you feel like forgiving, the more you probably need to do it. Remember, you're worth it! Here's a great question: 'Is it better to be happy, or right?'

So, how do you change the negative patterns that are driving your behaviours? Welcome to the **Personal Enlightenment and Release**

(PEAR) process – a system that guarantees to get you past your negative feelings and into a positive state …

The PEAR process takes the form of an imaginary conversation between you and the person who has caused you pain – and because while doing it you'll naturally and automatically find yourself in a slightly altered state of consciousness, what seems odd when you read about it makes perfect sense when you actually do it! And don't worry, an altered state of consciousness is much the same thing as day dreaming.

I first came across a version of this process when I decided to go for counselling – something I'd always turned my nose up at! (It only happened because a very cool, calm, collected male friend of mine decided to have a couple of counselling sessions himself. After a month or so when I bumped into him again, I noticed that he was even more cool, calm and collected – and I decided there and then that I wanted whatever he was on!)

My beloved grandfather had died six months previously and the counsellor had suggested that before I could move on, 'I needed to let my grandfather go'. There was nothing I wanted to do less. After all, the memories were all that I had left.

The counsellor was pretty insistent, and because he seemed to have his heart in the right place (and if I'm really honest, I thought that it would speed things up if I simply agreed with him!) I went along with his suggestions. We started the 'letting go' process and I was directed to have an imaginary conversation with my grandfather – and worse, I had to do it out loud, apparently because my subconscious mind would be better able to believe in what I was doing. I felt both self-conscious and foolish, but only for the first minute or so. It wasn't long before I really started to get into it, and I soon found myself sobbing my heart out.

There were a number of steps to the process – culminating in the decision that I had to make to let him go. The counsellor asked me to imagine my grandfather walking away from me and over the brow of a hill, out of sight. I thought my heart was going to break. As the session came to an end, I felt bone tired but strangely peaceful. When I got home it was early evening and I went straight to bed, sleeping solidly until noon the next day. When I awoke everything seemed different. Not only did I feel as though I was really alive for the first time in ages, but I was also able to picture my grandfather alive too, when previously, I'd been continually accompanied by the nightmare of him lying on his deathbed.

I sensed that something had completely changed in my life. What I had been through was not only powerful – but in my case life-changing, as I knew that I wanted to be able to help people in the same way that I'd been helped. In a paradoxical way, my grandfather's death had helped me see what I wanted to do with the rest of my life. Later that day, I called the counsellor and asked him to teach me what he knew.

Following is the five-step process that over the years, I've adapted and enhanced according to the needs and experiences of my own clients. The process works for all negative patterns and problems within relationships …

The PEAR (Personal Enlightenment and Release) process:

1 Expression of anger, hurt or grief

2 Forgiveness

3 Acceptance

4 Unconditional love

5 Letting go

1 Expressing anger, grief and hurt

Often we tend to bottle up our anger and hurt, with the result that it creates a 'pressure cooker' effect on our minds and bodies. As we don't want to look at the cause of our pain, we seek to avoid it. Yet by burying these feelings deep inside, we're not stopping them from affecting us. While anger, grief and hurt aren't negative feelings in themselves, when they're unresolved, they start to turn bad, causing us to become bitter. And it's the bitterness that gets us by eating away at our 'essence' which affects not only our personality but also our behaviours. Worse, over time, anger, hurt and grief that remain unexpressed tend to leak out into our physical bodies, causing us physical pain. Psychosomatic pain is very real, although it has tended to be a term used to dismiss someone's pain as 'just being in the mind.' A better description for psychosomatic pain would be 'pain that *originates* either in the mind or soul'.

Sadly, in today's culture, we're usually encouraged not to express our feelings. Think about it for a moment: when someone is visibly upset, the first thing we do is to try to stop them crying by trying to make them laugh! While I'm all for seeing the funny side to life, there does come a point when sadness has to be acknowledged and *felt*. When people cry around us it tends to make us feel bad, which is why we do all we can to cheer someone up. Less selfish behaviour though, would suggest that we encourage someone to express their feelings.

You might also want to note that if someone else's sadness triggers you to feel the same way, then you're also storing some unresolved pain of your own. You can only get triggered by other people's feelings if you harbour similar ones yourself.

However, it's also important to recognise that the expression of our pain is only the first stage in the process towards resolution. Simply stirring up feelings that make us feel bad is pointless, we'll just feel worse. In fact, wallowing in self-pity guarantees to turn you into a victim faster than Superman can change his clothes!

Be aware though, that you can't avoid the first stage of the PEAR process in a bid to avoid feeling pain. Feeling – and expressing – is the very necessary first step in the emotional healing process!

2   Forgiveness
Unfortunately, forgiveness isn't something that just washes over you after a certain period of time has elapsed. In fact, time really isn't a healer. Forgiveness is the healer and forgiveness is a decision. Only we can make that decision. And it's only when we decide to forgive others – or indeed ourselves – that we become free from negativity and give ourselves the opportunity to grow. Until we choose to forgive, our negative feelings direct our behaviours – which in turn affect our energy. When we're harbouring negativity, it's as though there's a dark negative, 'cobwebby' energy around us which stops our inner light from shining!

Forgiveness isn't about condoning – and it's certainly not about turning the other cheek. We forgive in order to free ourselves. We can only affect ourselves through our anger and hurt, not anyone else. For example, while you could be seething with anger, the other person could be playing golf, blissfully unaware of your feelings. If you choose not to forgive – whether it's someone else or yourself – you condemn yourself to living in a constant state of unhappiness.

3   Acceptance
Again, acceptance is a decision. It means that we choose to accept what is, and what has been. It also means that we choose to look at the situation as it really is, without bringing our 'story' into it. Acceptance doesn't mean that we condone what happened – or that we shouldn't do all we can to ensure the same scenario doesn't occur again in the future. And it's absolutely not about making ourselves into doormats for other people! Forgiveness and acceptance go hand in hand, enabling us to jump clear of the negative ties of resentment and anger. Indeed, as we become increasingly comfortable with ourselves, we'll be more inclined to prevent people from treating us badly.

4   Love

As the Beatles would teach us, 'All you need is love!' Love is the great healer. Remember, the opposite of love isn't hate, but fear. All of our negativity arises through the ego's fears – and love is the antidote! The kind of love I'm talking about isn't of the hearts and flowers variety, but is to do with forgiving, accepting and appreciating someone for all of who they are, even if their behaviours aren't the ones we'd adopt ourselves. This kind of love is unconditional and non-judgemental. When we love unconditionally, we want the best for the other person and have no envy or jealousy for their success. Unconditional love is the prerequisite for happiness, never mind enlightenment! If we all adopted an attitude of unconditional love, there'd be no wars, no conflict, and no poverty. As the adage goes, 'To heal the world all you need do is heal yourself.' I'd add that healing only occurs with the salve of unconditional love.

5   Letting go

The final step is to let go – which is, once again, a decision. We can't change the past but we can change how we *feel* about the past. Simply deciding to let go of our negativity isn't always easy but it is the only way to liberate our psyche! When we let go of negative memories, we're no longer driven by them – leaving us free to focus our energy on achieving our life ambitions, rather than wasting our time being bitter about the past.

As with many things in life, the first time is the hardest and the PEAR process in no exception. It's not that the work itself is hard, it's just that it feels like an alien way to go about things. But once you've applied the process to a particular situation, you'll feel so fantastic that you won't look back. Rather than jump in at the deep end, I suggest that you try the process in connection with a not-too-serious conflict, just to get the hang of it. (Of course, I should say at this juncture, that if you're suffering from serious mental health issues, you really must register with your doctor or other appropriate professional.) And remember, each step of the process is vital – don't be tempted to skip a step.

This process doesn't just work for dealing with relationship issues in the past – but it can also be used to help you deal with potential difficulties in the future too. If you're facing a situation with someone who somehow always knows which buttons to press, just by using the PEAR process in advance, you can take the sting out of their poisoned arrows. (Make no mistake, at first they'll still fire the arrows but instead of hitting you straight in the solar plexus, they'll sail straight over your head! After a while, sensing there's no fun in pressing your buttons any more, they'll simply scratch their heads in bewilderment and leave you alone.)

USING THE PROCESS WITH YOURSELF …

Sometimes it's us that we need to forgive more than anyone else. We tend to give ourselves far harsher sentences than a court would ever dish out. Guilt and a sense of personal shame – together with our anger at finding ourselves less than perfect – prompt us to begin an ongoing cycle of self-flagellation.

When I first started studying this kind of stuff, I had to undergo a form of the PEAR process myself. I was given a mirror to look into and told to 'talk to the person in the mirror as though it was another person.' At first I thought the facilitator was simply, well, simple – but I gave it a go and soon got into it. If I'm honest, I found it really hard to look myself in the eyes – but by the time I'd forgiven myself for past mistakes it got easier. And by the end of the process, I was able to look at myself – possibly for the first time in my life – and see that I wouldn't mind having someone like me as a friend!

It's fascinating how good we are at burying those things which really cause us to feel ashamed, as I was to find out when a friend asked me to take her through the PEAR process in a bid to stop the self-sabotage that she seemed to be continually experiencing in her life. To my surprise, when we had got to the end of the session, she'd not shed a single tear. I was perplexed and told her so.

'Well actually', she replied, 'I found the whole exercise really easy. I mean, the only thing that I'd never be able to forgive myself for was the abortion …' and as she said the word 'abortion', her hand flew up to her mouth.

It transpired that she'd never told a soul about the abortion. When we reapplied the PEAR process to the abortion, the tears certainly flowed then! Over the next few weeks and months, she completely blossomed – free from all the guilt that had been weighing her down for so long.

Section 2

FREE! FREE! FREE!

*When you know that you're more than just a physical body,
you've got a real head start in life*

Chapter 9

Discovering the amazing power of the subconscious mind!

*I*t had been a couple of weeks since we'd all last met – and I guess for each of us, there was a kind of trepidation. None of the delegates really knew what to expect – and I too was nervous; after all, these people held my future in their hands!

After helping ourselves to the coffee and doughnuts that awaited our arrival, we all settled down and a hush descended upon the room. The room was sunny and the table – the classic u-shape – was covered in a starched white linen tablecloth. In front of each delegate's place was one of my shiny, professionally printed manuals, a couple of sharpened pencils and a glass of sparkling water. I knew that the manuals wouldn't get read until well after the course, when the delegates would want to explore in greater depth all that they'd experienced on the action-packed two day programme – but for now the setting was probably pretty much as the delegates had expected. However, I – and some of the delegates judging from their comments after their initial one-to-one session – knew that this would be a course like no other they'd ever experienced.

Taking a deep breath, I started to speak. 'Welcome to the second stage in the Be Your Own Guru programme.'

A nervous smile played on the lips of a couple of the delegates and I continued, 'I know many of you have been through training before and if you're anything like me, you'll probably absolutely detest role-play, which is why we won't be doing any. And I know you've not been told much about the programme, nor been given anything to prepare and that's deliberate, as I wanted you all to keep an open mind. As you can see, I've not come armed with PowerPoint and while there's a structure to these two days, you'll be doing a lot of the directing and setting the pace – not me. After all, I'm here for you – not the other way round … We've got a lot to squeeze into just two days, so you're going to have to listen fast! Finally, the really good news is that we're going to be spending the next two days studying the most precious and interesting thing in the world – YOU!'

Knowing that I needed to start the session with something that was going to grab their attention, I slowly looked around the room and asked, 'Who would like to see just how powerful their subconscious mind is?'

A couple of hands shot up in the air. The others smiled, perhaps feeling relieved that they weren't going to have to volunteer at this early stage of the proceedings.

*'Actually, in a moment, you're **all** going to get the chance to find out! But before we do that, having spoken to you all individually, I want to find out exactly what each of you wants to get out of our two days together. So, split into pairs, and in three minutes I'm going to ask you to introduce your partner, tell us something about them that nobody knows and, finally, reveal to the rest of us what they want to get out of the programme.'*

Immediately everyone started talking animatedly to the person on one or other side of them, hurriedly gleaning the answers to the questions.

'OK, 30 seconds left … Right, who's going first?'

Grabbing a fat red felt tip marker, I walked up to the flip chart in the room and wrote in capital letters on the top of the first page:

'WHAT WE WANT TO GET OUT OF THE COURSE!'

Underneath, as the delegates started introducing each other and what they wanted to get out of the course, I began to write on the flip chart.

By the end of the two day session I want to know how to:

1   Say 'no' to people

2   Manage my time better

3   Make my relationships work better

4   Make people like me

5   Manage my anger better

6   Get on in my career

7   Deal with stress

8   Avoid making the same mistakes over and over again

9   Have fun!

'Well, congratulations, judging by that list – you're all on the right course!' I laughed, 'So, without further ado, let's get on with finding out how strong your subconscious mind is. This is where you start to get some exercise! Stand up, and find somewhere in the room where you can move around without hitting the person next to you.'

At this point, I stood on a chair. Not only did the extra height give me a little more authority but the unexpected sight of me throwing off my shoes and leaping on to the seat helped add theatricality to the occasion. 'Right, we're going to do the exercise three times. First, we're going to do it in reality, then we're going to do it in our imagination and then we're going to do it again in reality.

'So, what I want you to do is bring your outstretched right arm up in front of you and look down your arm as though you were looking down the barrel of a gun. Great. Now, I want you to bring your right arm round to the right and see how far you can comfortably reach. That's good. Is that as far as you can go? Good, go as far as you can go and when you have, make a mental note of how far you've gone on the wall, or the window behind you. Excellent. Now bring your right arm back down to your side.

'Relax. Now we're going to do the exercise in the imagination only, which means that you'll remain completely still. You'll probably find it easiest to do it with your eyes closed. First, closing your eyes helps you to get into your imagination more easily by shutting out any external stimuli and second, if you're concerned that you look silly, you don't need to worry as everyone else with have their eyes shut as well!'

A small ripple of laughter greeted my comment and it was clear that everyone was already beginning to feel more relaxed. It wouldn't be long before they were actively enjoying the session.

'Now', I continued. 'I want you to imagine that, once again, you bring your right arm up in front of you … just like you did last time.'

Noticing that one of the younger male delegates had started to raise his arm, I said in a slighter louder voice, 'And you're working in your imagination only, standing completely still.'

*But the young man continued to physically raise his arm, prompting me to leap off the chair and over to where he was standing. Gently, I put my hand on his arm and pushed it down to his side. 'Just in the **imagination**, I said.' By now, everyone was laughing, not so much **at** the delegate but more **with** him.*

Continuing with my instructions, I said, 'In the imagination only, bring your right arm up in front of you, just as you did last time. Now watch, as you move your right arm round to the right … and see how easily you reach your original point on the wall or window or whatever it was that was behind you. Good. Notice how flexible you feel as you now see yourself going one inch, two inches, four inches, wow – six inches past that original point. But you know that you are even more flexible, so you choose to move even further round to the right … nine inches, eleven inches – hey, more than a foot past that original point. Now imagining that you have all the flexibility of an owl, which as you know can turn its head 360°, and apply that same flexibility to yourself as you watch yourself moving fourteen, sixteen nearly eighteen inches past that original point on the wall or the window. And know, right now, that you're flexible enough to be able to bring your right arm even further, to nearly two feet past that original point on the wall!

'Great. Now, again in your imagination, bring your right arm back down to the side. Eyes open and yes, you've guessed it – we'll now do the exercise again in reality!

'So … bring your right arm up in front of you, look down your arm as though you're looking down the barrel of a gun … and bring your right arm round to the right and see just how much further you're capable of going past the original point on the wall or the window behind you …'

Laughter mixed in with amazement and excited chatter took over. With only once exception, everyone had managed to move a lot further after the visualisation!

Jenny, normally pretty timid, was doubled up with laughter, repeating over and over again, 'That's incredible, that's really amazing.'

'Wow, why does that work?' said Matt, who'd been more than a little surprised to find that he'd gone more than two feet further round.

'Take a seat, and I'll explain!' I replied.

Waiting for Jenny as she poured herself a glass of water, I then started to explain about the mind/body connection.

'Basically, as one of the forefathers of personal development, Napoleon Hill taught us, whatever the mind can conceive and believe, it can achieve. Also the subconscious mind does not readily distinguish between vivid imagination and reality. Let me explain. Your mind knew what was expected because it saw you do it when we first did the exercise. When you did the exercise in your imagination, your mind knew that the muscles in your back would have to relax if you were to go further round. And the magical thing is that your mind was able to relax those muscles in your spine, so that when you did the exercise again in reality, you were able to go much further round. How amazing is that!'

Everyone was nodding, apart from Pete who was shaking his head. 'But I didn't go further round, why's that? Aren't my mind and body connected like everyone else's?'

'Of course they are', I was quick to reassure him. 'While most people find it easy to "see" things in their imagination, some people simply find that rather than "seeing" they tend to "feel" or simply "know". There's no right or wrong way, it's just the way we're wired, that's all. In fact, that's an important point for us all to be aware of. Just because we perceive things differently doesn't make any of us right or wrong – just different. You'll be finding out a lot more about our differences and similarities – and the havoc they can cause – throughout the programme.'

Matt started to grin. This was absolutely the kind of thing he'd wanted to find out more about.

'OK, we'll be looking further into the mind/body connection a little later on, but for now I want us to spend a little time understanding more about the subconscious mind.'

Points to ponder as you start to …
Be your own guru

1 This is a great 'dinner party' exercise! You might find it easier to do this first with a friend, with one of you reading out the instructions and the other performing the exercise. Alternatively, you could record the instructions for yourself. Before you begin, make sure that you allow enough space around you to avoid hitting anyone or anything …

  Bring your outstretched right arm up in front of you and look down your arm as though you were looking down the barrel of a gun. Now, bring your right arm round to the right and see how far you can comfortably reach. Make a mental of how far you've gone on the wall, or the window behind you. Bring your right arm back down to your side. Next, do the exercise in your imagination only, which means that you keep completely still. It's easier with your eyes closed. In your imagination, bring your right arm up in front of you … just like you did last time. In your imagination, watch as you move your right arm round to the right … and see how easily you reach your original point on the wall or window. Notice how flexible you feel as you now see yourself going one inch, two inches, four inches, six inches past that original point. Know that you're even more flexible and choose to go even further round to the right … nine inches, eleven inches, more than a foot past the original point. Now imagine that you have all the flexibility of an owl, which as you know can turn its head 360°, and applying that same flexibility, see yourself moving fourteen, sixteen, nearly eighteen inches – nearly two feet – past that original point on the wall or the window. In your imagination, bring your right arm back down to the side.

  Open your eyes and repeat the exercise again in reality. Bring your right arm up in front of you, look down your arm as though you're looking down the barrel of a gun … and bring your right arm round to the right and see just how much further you're capable of reaching past the original point on the wall or the window behind you!

2 Get your thinking more positive … Wear an elastic band for a fort-night – and 'ping' it every time you have a negative thought. While the elastic band isn't magic, it'll help remind you, and keep you consciously aware of, your thoughts. You'll be amazed at just how much negative thinking you indulge in each and every day – all of which is negatively affecting your experiences in life. Remember – be very careful what you spend your time thinking about!

3 Take one of your SMART goals and practice imagining how it would feel to bring it into reality. See how it looks to be success-ful and feel the excitement and pure pleasure that achievement brings. Enjoy the feelings of celebration and bring the images and sensations to mind as often as you can throughout the days, weeks, months and years.

4 List your limiting beliefs. Think back to your childhood – what were the most common reprimands that you used to hear? Ponder over the next few days which of these beliefs are still affecting your life today. Decide which beliefs are useful to you and which are limiting you and dump the ones that aren't enhancing your life!

5 Who are you playing the 'blame game' with? Remember, every time you blame someone, you're not shifting responsibility, you're giving your power away.

Chapter 10

Getting to grips with what makes you tick

Your mind is far more than your brain. In fact, according to the ancient Egyptians, your mind resided in your heart, while your liver was the seat of your soul! Different beliefs have abounded through the ages. The early Greeks recognised the importance of the brain, but thought that it was the home of the soul rather than the intellect. The concept of the intellectual mind emerged in the seventeenth century, when the brain was recognised as being an organ of intelligence.

But as well as the brain and the mind to get our heads around, we also need to get to grips with the conscious and subconscious mind, as well as the differences in thinking between our left and right brains …

Let's start with the latter first. The concept of left and right brain thinking was first introduced to an unsuspecting world in the late 1960s by American psycho-biologist Roger W. Sperry who was to be awarded a Nobel Prize in 1981. The left brain, he argued, is analytical, verbal and sequential, while the right brain is visual, intuitive and creative. Research into the subject was later to prove that things weren't quite as simple as Sperry had made out, but nevertheless it's a model that works – at least on a superficial level – and which has found increasing popularity. This can be seen from the fact that we tend to label rigid, rational types as 'left brainers' and artistic, hippy types as 'right brainers'. Personally, I think we should focus on introducing unity into the situation – at worst we'd be blessed with a world full of colourful accountants!

IT'S YOUR SUBCONSCIOUS MIND THAT MAKES YOU A SURVIVOR …

When we get into what we call an emotional hijack, it's the primitive part of our brain – the amygdala – that's to blame. The amygdala processes and interprets our emotions and evolution has given it a good nose for anything that threatens our survival. As we've seen earlier, its primary orientation is around our physical survival and whenever it senses something that could hurt us, it releases adrenaline and a bunch of other stress hormones that help us prepare for flight or fight.

> **Guru Success Tip**
>
> Remember that it's what's inside our heads that makes us stressed – not outside events!

The problem though, is that the amygdala is unable to distinguish between the previously mentioned sabre-toothed tiger and a hyperventilating office manager – either way, our bodies are still drenched in hormones dedicated to ensure our survival. Once the hormones – especially adrenaline – are released, we're unable to resort to rational thought because everything that isn't absolutely necessary for our imminent survival is simply shut down. It's not only the more sophisticated elements of our brains – like the cortex which is responsible for rational thought and our ability to judge and cogitate – that are switched off, but our digestive systems are stopped and our heart and breathing rates increase to increase the delivery of oxygen to our muscles.

We feel the intensity of emotion – whether we're responding to a threat or intense pleasure – and release the appropriate hormones before our rational cortex gets a look-in. It's for this reason that we 'fly off the handle' (others perceive our reactions as 'over the top' and inappropriate) or, in the case of intense pleasure, we become addicted to things that we know rationally are no good for us!

MAKING UP YOUR MINDS IS FAR EASIER TO SAY THAN DO ...

It was Sigmund Freud who first likened our minds to an iceberg (see the graphic below). He suggested that the visible tip of the iceberg represents the conscious mind (the bit that gets you up in the morning), while the invisible part under the waterline (the dangerous bit that that brought down the Titanic) represents the subconscious mind.

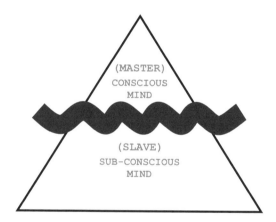

When we live from our conscious mind, we're aware of who we are, what we're doing and why we're doing it. The conscious mind is the part of us that determines our goals – and puts in place a strategy for their achievement. The subconscious mind not only maintains bodily functions without you being aware of them (when was the last time you focused on making your heart beat?) but it also stores and organises memories – together with the emotions you felt at the moment the events in the memory occurred.

The subconscious has a number of prime objectives:

- It runs the body

- It stores and organises memories

- It maintains and generates habits

- It is the domain of the emotions

- It controls and maintains all perceptions

Our subconscious mind views life through the filters it has built up through experience and stored as memory. However, our mental filters are not necessarily based in truth but are the result of our personal understanding of that truth. This explains why two people can interpret the same scenario in completely different ways! When they're not clouded by negative or unreal perceptions, our filters enable us to get through the day. Without being able to take some things for granted, we'd never have the time or energy to progress. Think about it for a moment: every time you stood on a different floor for the first time, you'd have to test its strength and make sure that it wouldn't collapse under your weight. We do more than survive – we prosper and grow – because of the mind's filtering systems. Without them we'd have to go back to square one every day.

Our brains need to filter information; if they didn't, we would go insane due to 'information overload'. In order to make sense of the world around us, we use only a tiny percentage of the information available – and the information we choose is dependent on a number of factors including:

- Values

- Beliefs

- Memories

- Attitudes

- Self talk

The trouble starts however, when our filtering systems become distorted. This usually happens because what we *feel* taints our sensory perceptions. Unless we're consciously aware of our feelings, we find ourselves unable to distinguish between them and our thoughts, and when we turn them into memory they tend to become even more blurred. Distorting our perceptions in this way is similar to wearing a pair of eye glasses with wrong prescription lenses – everything looks fuzzy and distorted!

The subconscious mind tends to be very visual – with most of our memories being recalled as images. However, most of us are also able to store the memories – and the feelings we associated with them – in connection with sound too. A certain authoritative speaking voice can have us quaking like jellies in no time if it has the same ring as that of a dreaded school teacher!

Traditionally, the subconscious mind has been likened to a slave. This is partly because it tends to work on the principle of least effort (and needs repeated reminders for long term projects!) and partly because it works hard to bring into reality whatever it is that you spend your time thinking about. Unfortunately, the subconscious is not programmed to distinguish between what's good and what's bad for us. It just believes that if you're thinking about it, then it must be what you want!

If the subconscious is the slave, then who's running the show? The conscious mind plays the role of 'master' to the subconscious mind's 'slave'. The conscious mind is where you decide what you want to achieve, what your priorities are and also, what you're going to have for lunch! If you're clear on all of these and remain focused on the images they inspire, your subconscious mind will do the rest.

This is where goals come in. In order to do what it was born to do, your conscious mind should be thinking in terms of goals – SMART (Specific, Measurable, Achievable, Ritten, Timed) goals. It also helps if you can get it to work out an action plan, but if not, just regularly visualising the goal will help the subconscious mind see that you're serious and get it started in manifesting your goal.

WHILE IT MAY ALL SOUND TOO GOOD TO BE TRUE ...

You'll be pleased to know that a long while back, I put the whole SMART goals thing to the test. A former colleague of mine was reading a magazine over lunch when she became really excited by a feature on the subject of goal manifesting.

'It's really easy', she exclaimed. 'All we need do is to think about what we want – and our subconscious minds will do all the rest.'

'Yeah right!' was my instant reaction.

'No, listen', she said even more insistently. 'All we have to do is make a written list of our goals, work out an action plan for achieving them and just sit back and wait.'

It seemed hard to believe but to be fair nothing else seemed to be working for me at the time. And now that she'd mentioned an action plan, it did seem a little more feasible. Not wanting to pour cold water on her enthusiasm, I decided to play along. I felt it would be easier to measure the success of her suggestions if I chose a material goal – at least I'd be able to see whether or not I'd achieved it! I'm not particularly materialistic but as my car wasn't in the best state of repair, I decided that this would be a good area of my life to choose for the goal setting experiment. And because I used to enjoy sailing with my grandfather as a child, I also decided that I wanted to recreate that 'wind in the hair' factor, so nothing less than a convertible car would do!

The fact that I had no spare cash at the time – and nor were my personal circumstances likely to change at any point in the near future – didn't deter me. No, if this goal thing was going to work, then it was going to have to work on my terms. Having made the decision about the car, I then set about making an action plan. This became very detailed and I thought that if I played my cards right, I'd probably be able to afford a very old convertible in about eight years time. Hardly the stuff of dreams but nevertheless, I would at least be able to pride myself on having achieved the 'A' in SMART (Achievable)! Once we'd written down our musings, I put the scrappy piece of paper in my top desk drawer and didn't give it too much conscious thought. Little did I realise it but my subconscious mind was repeatedly being reminded of my aspirations every time I opened the drawer and saw that piece of paper.

A couple of months later, I went to see a local garage owner who I thought might take some advertising space in my business magazine. Out of the blue, after we'd signed the deal, he happened to mention that his own blue BMW convertible was up for sale.

'Would you be interested in buying it?' he asked casually.

'Well, of course I would', I replied. 'But frankly, I don't have that kind of money.'

'How about taking a loan?' he'd responded.

Shrugging my shoulders, I said, 'I don't think that would work. I'm self-employed and at the moment, I don't own my home. Sadly, I won't be able to tick all the boxes on a loan form.'

At that, the garage owner had simply smiled and said that I shouldn't worry about that – he sat on the committee that approved the loans!

One problem down – one to go! Even knowing I could get a loan, I also knew that I wouldn't have enough money each month to service it. Just at that moment, something clicked inside me. Intuitively, I knew that if only I could see how, that car *could* be mine. I didn't know it then, but I was beginning to use the power of being my own guru!

'Right, give me two days and I'll put my subconscious mind to work on the problem. I'm serious. Don't sell that car to anyone else, promise?'

He promised and I got back into my own car, wondering whether perhaps this time, I really had lost it. I tried to think of a plan on the way home but nothing came to me. It wasn't long before I fell back into my what-was-then-usual negative pattern, thinking how stupid I'd been, imagining that I could have had a car like that anyway.

The next morning when I woke up though, it was a different story. A solution suddenly hit me between the eyes. Yes, I was self-employed – so why didn't I turn that into a plus rather than a minus? At the time, I was working for three organisations on a part time, self-employed basis. Had I been working for any one of them, then the job would have come with a company car. I'd had a company car in my previous job, so I knew I was being realistic. I'd not upped my fees in a while, so perhaps it was time for a serious conversation.

I quickly made an appointment with the first of my clients and, knowing him pretty well, I told him the whole story. 'I think that if I worked for you full time, you'd provide me with a car, wouldn't you?'

'Yes, I'm sure we would', he replied half resignedly, half laughing. 'But I'm not about to give you a car now, you know!'

'No, of course not. But, as my work for you takes up about a third of my time, how would you feel about providing me with a third of a car? You know I haven't put up my fees for a while, despite doing a lot more work for you than I was in the beginning …'

He smiled again – both at the audacity of my suggestion and also in acknowledgement of the truth that I was indeed doing much more work for his company than either of us had originally anticipated. Between us we agreed that his organisation would pay a third of the car loan repayment – and that I'd sort out the paperwork, tax and insurance. We shook hands on the deal, both of us knowing that it was fair.

> **Guru Success Tip**
>
> Make sure that as you cruise through life, you look for the opportunities and don't just try to avoid the obstacles!

I was ecstatic! With one client in the bag, I went on to have the same discussion with the other two. Knowing that someone else had agreed to the deal, the others were happy to follow suit.

Within the self-imposed two day deadline, I rang my garage owner and told him that if he could still organise the loan, then I'd be able to repay it. The rest, as the say, is history and it was only a matter of days before I was driving my pride and joy – a bright blue, convertible BMW!

Apart from learning about the power of the subconscious mind – and to listen to my colleague more carefully in future – I also understood about the power of goals from my experiment. Because 'convertible car' was on my list of goals, when an opportunity to acquire one arose, my subconscious antennae were on full alert and started to get very creative. If I hadn't listed 'convertible car' as my goal, then although exactly the same opportunity would still have arisen, I'd have turned it away, thinking that there was no way that I could have a car like that!

The opportunities for what we want are always there, but we don't spot them unless we're very clear about what it is that we want. Taking time out to focus our minds on what we want is therefore invaluable.

The second thing I learned from my 'goal experiment' was that once you attain a goal, you should replace it with a new one. I've never done that with the car which is why, on my driveway, you'll still see a now very old – but much loved – blue BMW convertible!

LET YOUR SUBCONSCIOUS TAKE THE STRAIN …

Once we've mastered a new skill – driving for example – we don't actively think about it any more, instead we entrust it to the subconscious mind, which performs as though it's on automatic pilot. (Before you get scared and think that the roads are full of drivers who are not consciously aware of what they're doing, you should also know that being on 'automatic pilot' is a very safe place to be, not least because even though you're not aware of it, your senses are heightened knowing that they must protect you even when 'you're not all there'!)

Actually, we're all in a light state of trance or altered state of consciousness every 1½ hours or so – if we weren't, we'd go mad. Have you ever driven a routine trip and then found yourself not able to remember the journey when you arrived? Well, you were in a light state of self-hypnosis. Our minds need to tune out in this way on a regular basis to avoid 'external stimuli overload'.

Where it all goes wrong …

Frighteningly, few of us have a clear idea of where we're headed, let alone have goals – which means that without the conscious mind playing its role of master, we tend to default to the workings of the subconscious mind. This, as my friend Ian would have it, is like 'inviting the lunatics to run the asylum'!

For some unfathomable reason, human beings appear to be hard wired to default to negative thinking unless positive thoughts are consciously introduced. Once again, we see the rationale for having SMART goals. And remember, the subconscious mind acts as the slave to our conscious mind – and its only role is to bring into reality whatever it is that we're thinking about. Imagine the chaos if you don't have any positive goals on which to focus – all your time will be spent worrying, and worse, your subconscious mind will be hard at work doing its best to manifest your worries into reality.

How do I know this? Sadly, because it's what I used to do! While it might seem strange for someone who's regularly hired as a motivational speaker, I really used to be 'Miss Negative'. I'm blessed in that I was born with a very powerful and vivid imagination but it's only now that I can see how I used it to shoot myself in the foot. Money – or rather the lack of it – was always an issue for me. I used to spend (for 'spend', read 'waste') a great deal of time worrying about not being able to pay the bills – and guess what happened in reality?

Actually, in reality, I did always manage to get the bills paid – not least because I had another mental programme running which said that, like other business people I admired at the time, I'd always be able to 'pull the white rabbit out of the hat at the 11th hour'. And I did just that. Again and again. You can just hear my subconscious mind saying, 'Strange, I can't understand why you'd want to create such stress for yourself but clearly you want to because it's what you're spending your time thinking about. OK, let's set about making it happen for you!' It took me years to work out that I was responsible for the kind of life (and for 'life' read 'existence') that I was experiencing – and that if I wanted to change my experiences then I had to get to grips with *changing my thinking*! I was forced to realise that the subconscious mind makes a wonderful slave and an appalling master!

It was the same for my client Stephen who was bored and overweight when we first met. However, when he started to change his thinking and harness the power of his subconscious mind, he was amazed at how quickly he managed to manifest his dreams.

Together we'd explored Stephen's aspirations – as well as his childhood dreams. We'd agreed that not all goals should be material – but as he enjoyed a fairly happy home life, Stephen had decided to set himself a challenging goal that would give him a sense of purpose at work.

Like many boys, Stephen had been an enormous fan of James Bond and had boasted that one day he would own an Aston Martin like his childhood hero. However, everyday life had soon overshadowed his dreams and Stephen had become bogged down with earning enough money to pay the bills and keep a roof over his head. Worse, his self-belief had been severely knocked as a child when his father had laughed at his dreams of owning such a beautiful car. Patting Stephen on the head, his father had told him to remember his station in life, 'Everyone in our family has always had to work hard just to survive – don't you expect to be any different.'

In order for Stephen to succeed, it was obvious that he was going to have to re-programme his subconscious mind. Firstly, he would need to delete his father's negative thought patterns. In order to do that, Stephen had to accept that his father had only been trying to protect him. Secondly, Stephen needed to forgive his father – whose beliefs he could now see had held him back in many areas for most of his life. By forgiving his father, Stephen was not condoning his actions, but was merely untying himself from the negative energy that had been weighing him down.

After letting go of his father's thought patterns, Stephen was now free to create the goals to which he aspired. I'd explained to him that there was a big difference between wishful thinking and clearly defined SMART goals. Looking more enthused than he had for a while, Stephen had decided to focus his attention on achieving his SMART goal of a silver Aston Martin within three years. As well as the streamlined beauty of the vehicle itself, Stephen had chosen the Aston Martin because of its personal symbolism to him.

I spent a while showing Stephen how to powerfully visualise his goal as well as encouraging him to really get into feeling the excitement of owning his dream car. At the end of our session, he promised to spend ten minutes each day imagining the pleasure of owning and driving the Aston Martin. As well as seeing himself as another person sitting in the driving seat, he also learned to picture the view through the wind-screen, as though he was really there!

Of course, simply imagining his dream coming true wouldn't have been enough to bring the Aston Martin into reality. So Stephen and I spent a session creating an action plan that would enable Stephen to generate sufficient cash. He knew that the enterprise would require hard work but with his new set of beliefs in place, he really believed that he could make a go of the new business concept that he'd been toying with for the last year or so. While Stephen may have had a mere pipe dream before, the difference now was that he had self-belief – and he'd programmed his mind to believe that he could succeed. Previously, he'd been programmed to believe that he could never succeed – and that he and his family were destined to struggle.

Fast forward to three years later … and Stephen was once more in my office. But this time, I was sitting opposite an enthusiastic, slim and vibrant individual. Stephen proudly told me that he had dropped into my office to take me out to lunch – in his new silver Aston Martin DB9!

> **Guru Success Tip**
>
> Use your mind to help you manifest your dreams – visualise your goal becoming reality. What will it look like, how will you feel?

USE THE MAGIC OF GOALS TO ENHANCE YOUR LIFE …

Focus and intention are the lifeblood of the subconscious mind. As we've already discovered, what you spend your time thinking about is what you create in your reality. All we need do to get the reality that we want, is to get better at employing the strategic abilities of the conscious mind, coupled with practicing our visualising skills. The easiest way to tone up the conscious mind is through setting SMART goals. Goals help our minds to focus on who we want to be – and on what we want to achieve.

We've already seen how the conscious and subconscious minds can be helped to work in harmony together. One of the easiest ways to achieve this is through the creation of SMART goals by the conscious mind, which provides the subconscious mind with a to-do list! The subconscious naturally defaults to doing the least possible, so without goals the mind will do its best to help you achieve nothing at best, or your negative worries at worst!

There's a huge amount of stuff out there on goals already – indeed the self-help bookshelves groan with tomes aimed at helping people create magnificent lives through power goals. But the strange thing is, even though everyone knows the power of goals, very few people actively use them. Extraordinary as it may seem, less than 10% of the population appear to have any goals at all, and the number dwindles dramatically when the question is posed about whether or not those goals are SMART! So, the good news is that if you want to join the elite, spend a little time working out some SMART goals for yourself and you'll find yourself automatically in the nation's top 10%!

People often say that they have 'tried' goals but that the process simply hasn't worked for them. The reason for this is pretty straightforward. Their goals have been pipe dreams – if your goals aren't SMART, then all you've got is a wish list. Smart people have SMART goals.

MAKING AN EFFECTIVE ACTION PLAN …

Once you're clear about your goals, indeed your purpose, the next stage is to create an action plan. It helps to think of your goal as the destination and your action plan as the map that will help you get there. To work out your action plan, it's easiest to work backwards. Visualise your goal being a reality, then rewind the video. What did you need to do in order to make the vision a reality? By breaking your big goal down into a series of 'mini-goals', you can create an effective action plan. To be really effective, it's good to start the action plan with something that you can get your teeth into right now – today – as this shows your subconscious mind that you're really serious about turning your goal into reality!

Finally, as I've sadly found out with my old but much-loved convertible, putting new goals in place when you've achieved the current one is vital if you're to become increasingly successful. Not doing this means that you'll tend to revert to default – you'll start again with the negative thinking. Taken to the extreme, not having new goals can bring you back to square one, as my clients Max and Sue very nearly discovered …

The couple glowered at each other over their tea and biscuits – each too disgusted with the other's behaviour over the Christmas period to be able to speak. Max and Sue had been married for five years – and both enjoyed high-powered jobs that provided matching salaries. The couple had gone skiing over the holiday period – and to their horror had discovered that all the romance in their relationship had long gone. Used to the concept of working with a coach to improve their careers, Sue suggested that the couple should find a similar guide to help them save their marriage. To her surprise, Max had readily agreed – preferring the more business-like approach of a coach to the touchy/feely image he had of a marriage counsellor.

When I asked the couple what had brought matters to a head, Sue quickly responded that Max's flirtatious behaviour with the chalet girls on their skiing holiday had made her feel rejected, jealous and unattractive.

Pointing out that jealousy in this instance was actually a good thing – because it meant that there were still feelings between the couple – I asked Sue whether Max had always been a flirt.

'Not at all', she answered. 'He only used to have eyes for me. But lately, he only talks about work and doesn't seem to be interested in me or what I am doing.'

Acknowledging that there are always two sides to the story, I turned to Max and asked him how he felt about the situation. His response came as no surprise. 'Our marriage was so good in the early days – but in the last couple of years we've become so focused on our work that there just doesn't seem to be any time for us any more.'

Max went on to admit that he felt Sue was much
more interested in her career than she was in
him. 'To be honest, yes, I was flirting on holiday
– but it wasn't because I was really interested in
those other women. It was more because they
made me feel good about *me*. They laughed at
my stories and seemed to be interested in what
I had to say – which is more than I can say for
Sue, who sometimes talks to me as though I am
one of her staff!'

As they each talked through the way they felt, both Max and Sue
started to relax because they were beginning to understand the root
of the problem, which meant there was every chance that it could be
solved. After taking the couple through the PEAR process – in which
they forgave each other for their hurtful behaviour – both agreed to
work on setting some goals and creating an action plan which would
get their marriage back on track.

With their major goal for the year being to rekindle their marriage, the
couple together started thinking about what they needed to do in order
for their dreams to manifest into reality. They agreed that for a start,
both would bring no work home at the weekends. Also, every Friday
or Saturday night, the couple planned to go for a romantic night out
– with each taking it in turns to organise the event. Laughing, they
both agreed that they were not to talk about their jobs!

Max also suggested that each quarter, the couple should go for a romantic weekend away – an idea that made Sue smile as she remembered
the early days of their courtship, when they'd visited several European
cities. Delighted with the progress they'd made, Sue proposed that the
couple should also come for quarterly marriage coaching sessions to
make sure that they both carried through their good intentions. Max
readily agreed. After putting dates in the diary, the couple – hand in
hand – left my office, looking like young lovers with a rosy future!

As well as saving their marriage, Max and Sue also proved that goals work equally well for non-material aspirations!

MAKING THE MOST OF YOUR POWERS OF VISUALISATION!

We have already seen how strong the subconscious mind is – and that it can't distinguish between vivid imagination and reality. To help your goals manifest more quickly, it helps if you can visualise the reality – *as though it's already happened.* This is known as the 'power of intention' and is the key to our success (or failure) in life. Remember, our subconscious minds work hard to bring into reality whatever we spend our time thinking about. If you're focused on struggling to reach your goal, or on how awful your life is because you haven't yet got what you want, then that's what your subconscious will manifest for you. But if you're focused on what you want out of life, you will eventually achieve it, even if it's not in the way you initially imagined. Because the subconscious mind processes its thinking literally, it's vital that you focus on what you want to achieve as though it has already happened. If you only think about what you want as an event that will happen at some point in the future, your subconscious will do all it can to make sure that it remains a possibility for the future, rather than something that can be achieved in the 'now'!

It also helps if you bring all your senses into play. For example – when you think about achieving your goal, what do you see? Now imagine it in glorious Technicolor! How does it feel, knowing that you've accomplished what you wanted? Where do you feel it in your body? Where do you feel the excitement? What can you hear? Is it other people congratulating you? Is there a piece of music that you associate with success? The more realistic – and exciting – you can make your visualisation the more quickly it will be achieved. Allow yourself to daydream regularly about your future successes – remembering to imagine that you've already achieved them.

Sometimes it's our fear of disappointment that gets in the way. Fearing that we won't get what we really want, we avoid thinking about success – in order to avoid the pain of not getting our own way. It's an easy trap to fall into – and one that I very nearly fell into with this book! All that stood between me and the book deal was the necessity of putting a proposal together. Rather than being thrilled at the opportunity, I was instead overwhelmed with negativity and anger. I couldn't understand why at first. But then I started to investigate my feelings and realised that it was my fear of not securing a book deal that was causing me to create behaviours that would enable me to avoid writing the proposal. Of course, this type of limiting behaviour would have ensured that I wouldn't have been able to make my dream come true – but (or so my subconscious mind would have had it) I would then have been able to blame myself for not writing the proposal – which would have been less painful than being rejected for not being good enough!

Guru Success Tip

Remain focused on the 'what' but remain open as to the 'how' – in this way you flow with the tide of co-creation!

Having recognised one of my deep seated patterns, I started visualising like crazy, imagining how I would feel to be told that I had secured what my soul really cherished, a real book deal! Within about half an hour I started to feel an ecstatic – bordering on electric – buzz of excitement. And the really crazy thing was that I managed to write the proposal in just three hours, quite an achievement when you consider that I'd been struggling to get something down on paper for the previous three weeks!

So, learn from my mistake – and give yourself permission to imagine achieving your heart's desire. That way, there's every chance that you'll succeed. Focusing on the disaster of failing simply guarantees failure. The Dutch have a great saying, 'You already start with a "no"' - meaning that by *doing* something, anything, you at least give yourself the chance of bettering your position.

As children, we're often brought up to believe that 'pride comes before a fall' or that 'a bird in the hand is worth two in the bush'. While nobody likes people who are arrogant or smug, it's easy to see how too much of this type of thinking can keep us small and fearful. It happened to a one-time client of mine, Derrick, whose childhood experiences stopped him believing in himself.

Derrick sounded tired and weary as he told me his career story. For the last twenty years he'd worked doggedly as a financial advisor and while he had managed to keep his head above water, financial freedom had always eluded him. Derrick had always held what he described as a healthy and cynical disregard for all forms of personal development – but having seen his son-in-law's salary outstrip his own, he had decided that he needed to do something to salve not only his pride but also ensure his own financial future.

I'd asked Derrick about his goals and aspirations – and while he had done some work in this area, it was clear that there were underlying beliefs from his childhood that were holding him back. While Derrick paid lip service to his goals – he didn't truly feel in his heart that they would ever be achievable.

As a child, Derrick had grown-up in a family that believed that life was a struggle. Not being made bankrupt was the family's goal – and each month Derrick's parents scrimped and saved in order to pay their bills. Spare cash was a rarity and Derrick had long ago learned that he shouldn't expect too much fun in life.

I told Derrick about the subconscious mind – and how it works as our slave to bring our thoughts into reality, without distinguishing whether our thoughts were actually good or bad for us. Whatever the mind can imagine and believe, it can create – so therefore it's vital for us to spend our time firmly focused on what we want, rather than on what we dread.

For all his life, Derrick's thoughts had been focused on poverty – but if he were to create prosperity in his life, then he would need to change his perspective. Together we worked on healing the past and creating positive goals for his future. We achieved this by helping Derrick make the necessary changes to the programmes he was running in his subconscious mind. Finally, Derrick and I discussed the difference between prosperity consciousness and wishful thinking.

> **Guru Success Tip**
>
> When you think about your goal, imagine it as though it has already manifested – this helps your subconscious line up with your sense of expectation and belief!

'It's all a matter of intention and expectation. If you're hoping for an abundant life but are secretly expecting – or fearing – failure, then you're setting yourself up for a lot of frustration and disappointment', I told him. 'However, if you create goals which you know are achievable – and which you can visualise happening, you are in a much stronger position. Curiously, even belief isn't enough – it's only when you really *know* and *feel* that your goal simply *has to become reality* that it will start to manifest. The important thing in life', I finished, 'is to remember to focus on what you want – rather than on what you don't want!'

Derrick had left my office with plenty to think about – and with an eager glint in his smiling eyes. I heard from him about nine months later – and already he'd earned more than he had in the whole of the previous year.

Using your imagination in this way is really pretty easy once you know how – and the great news is that we're all capable of it. Let me ask you a question. What colour is your sofa at home? See, it was easy to picture it! And if you need any further reassurance, you might like to know that when I was giving a talk once to a business group, one of the delegates was blind. She had no problem with the 'moving the arm' visualisation exercise whatsoever – both to her surprise and my amazement!

Finally, to answer a question that I'm often asked – you only have the power to create your *own* reality. Thinking negative thoughts about someone else will not cause them harm! However, you should be aware that the spiritual law of karma (we reap what we sow) will come into play if you attempt to harm someone, and the ill-will you *intend* for them will sooner or later rebound on you.

GETTING TO GRIPS WITH YOUR BELIEF SYSTEMS …

The subconscious mind not only acts as slave to the conscious mind, but it's also the storehouse for all our memories – and the emotions we felt at the time. Amazingly, those stored emotions are just as powerful as the day the event occurred. Emotions do not alter over time – or fade away. Indeed, because the subconscious seeks to protect us, it is also capable of repressing traumatic memories that are accompanied by unresolved negative emotions. But just because these negative emotions and memories are 'buried' doesn't mean they're not affecting us. Our beliefs form programmes that are also housed in the subconscious mind which in turn drive our behaviours – often in ways which we're not even aware of.

Some lucky children are brought up with empowering beliefs – and they believe that if they choose to, they can conquer the world! However, for most of us, the emphasis was on what we couldn't – or shouldn't – do.

Some of the most common beliefs that we were brought up on as children include:

- 'Nobody likes a show-off!'
  (Better not tell anyone about my abilities, as I'll be rejected)

- 'You're stupid, you'll never amount to anything!'
  (What's the point, I'll fail anyway)

- 'No one in our family has ever been rich'
  (It doesn't matter what I do, poverty is in my genes)

- 'You are not good enough, so you don't deserve nice things'
  (Good enough seems unreachable, so I can't have nice things)

- 'Pride comes before a fall'
  (I'd better not try, as things will be even worse afterwards)

What were you taught as a child that no longer serves you today?

As children, we tend to believe that those in authority have superior knowledge to us, and as a consequence we accept their comments without question. Of course, what may have been true in one instance doesn't necessarily hold true on all occasions – but because we've absorbed the command without question, we unwittingly behave accordingly. It's about time that we all realised that parents and teachers are simply the best hypnotists! Often the 'rules' which we live our lives by are no more than a reflection of other people's experiences. Until you start to investigate your beliefs consciously – and choose to let go of those that limit you – they'll continue to hold you back.

We can only begin to reprogramme our minds when we make the decision to take responsibility for our thoughts, our feelings and our behavioural patterns. However, the downside of making this decision is that by taking responsibility for ourselves, we can no longer indulge in the blame game. You know the type: 'If only they'd change, I'd be OK', or 'It's all my parents' fault, there's nothing I can do about it'. We feel that blame shifts responsibility on to the other person but remembering all the time we're blaming, we're giving our power away!

Chapter 11
Experiencing the mind/ body connection

*H*aving experienced the power of the subconscious mind for themselves, the delegates were eager to get on with learning more. While most of them had heard of SMART goals before, somewhat surprisingly, none of them had realised that without goals, the subconscious mind tends to default to negative thinking.

Just before the mid-morning coffee break, Jenny had a breakthrough moment. 'I used to have these big dreams as a child', she said. 'I wanted to be a doctor and make people better. But my family just laughed at me and told me that I wasn't clever enough. My big brother – who I worshipped – also said that I was silly to have such lofty ambitions because life would decide my fate, and that I wouldn't have a say in it.'

Jenny's sadness had been palpable. Her voiced lowered slightly as she continued, 'I remember the day when something seemed to die inside me – I think it was hope. Ever since, I've tended to accept what life has dished out to me. Sure, I've got a good job and a healthy family and while I should feel content *with that, somehow I'm just not. I feel that I have so much responsibility on my shoulders that there isn't any time or space for me. Somehow, I've got left out of the equation. Surely, there must be more to life?'*

Silence greeted Jenny's words.

'Before we go any further', I interrupted, 'are we all agreed that we keep any personal stuff that arises during the course absolutely between us?' Raising my right hand, I asked everyone who signed up to such an agreement to raise their hand too. Everyone's hand immediately shot up. 'Good, if you hadn't raised your hand I'd have had to ask you to leave!'

Turning to Jenny, I asked her how she felt now that she was seeing her family's – and particularly her brother's – advice in a different light.

A tear began to roll down her left cheek. 'I'm feeling a mixture of things: sadness, disappointment, anger. If only I'd had more belief in myself and hadn't listened to what they'd told me perhaps I'd have had a completely different career. A completely different life even!'

'Maybe it's not too late to retrain?', said a helpful voice from the other side of the table.

Jenny had shaken her head. 'That's kind of you to say but being realistic it's just not going to happen. I'm too old to start again in the education system and apart from that, my husband and I have got used to living on two incomes.'

While I didn't agree with Jenny's statement that she was 'too old', I completely understood that her current circumstances meant that she wasn't in a position to simply jack in her job and start again.

However, I very much believed that there was something salvageable from the situation. 'When you said that "as a child you wanted to make people better," what does that really mean?'

Pausing for a moment, Jenny said that she'd watched her grandmother suffer with a variety of illnesses. 'It was awful to see the pain etched on her face. I just wanted to be able to do something to help her.'

'OK, do you think that there would have been other ways in which she could have been helped, as well as by a doctor?'

'I'm not sure what you mean', she quickly replied.

'Well, we've been looking at the power of the subconscious mind – and you yourself were amazed at how much further round you were able to go when we did the arm exercise. Many of the ailments we experience are actually symptoms, but if you want to bring about lasting relief, then it's really about getting to the cause and dealing with it. There's a lot of research around that proves that disease – or dis-ease if you like – is first created by the negative thoughts and feelings that we hold on to over time. I know we're touching on an area that might seem a little outlandish for some of you but if you're interested, I can tell you a story or two about the experiences of some of my clients.'

'I'd certainly love to learn more', Jenny said. 'What about everyone else?' As everyone had nodded in agreement, Jenny had suggested that rather than have a full mid-morning break, they should just take five minutes and bring their coffee back to the room. 'Perhaps we could take the break now?'

In less than the allotted five minutes, all the delegates were back in their seats, eager to hear more. During the break, I'd caught up with Jenny and reassured her that even though she hadn't been able to make her childhood dreams come true, she still had plenty of opportunity to follow her heart now.

'There are many therapies that help clients feel better – anything from hypno-therapy to the more esoteric energy healing systems like Reiki. You could use the job you're in now to pay for your training – and then, depending on how

you feel at the end of your studies, you could practice either on a full- or part-time basis. We always have options, even if they're not always clear to us!'

It had been a lot for her to take on, but there was glint of hope in her eyes that I hadn't seen before. She could feel it too. Putting her hand on my arm, she thanked me – saying that she was really enjoying the course. 'Thank you, that's really kind of you', I replied, 'but don't forget that it's your boss you should really be thanking – it was he who had the foresight to put you on the course in the first place.'

Before launching into my real life case stories, I first explained a little about the mind/body connection. 'Our bodies are an excellent guidance system – particularly for people suffering with chronic illnesses and ailments. Curiously, the body tends to speak in puns – or at least reflect our colloquial language. For example, a great friend of mine has always talked about "people being a pain in neck" – and now, she is suffering from osteoporosis, in her neck! It's as though her neck had been physically storing the negative emotions she was feeling about different events in her life. And it was only when she started dealing with those negative emotions on a mental level, that her neck pain began to ease.

'Remember our friend the subconscious mind? As you now know, it's the domain of our emotions – and these can be stored anywhere within our bodies, not just the brain. Generally, as we go through life we're not consciously aware of our memories or the feelings we've attached to them – and the effect they can have on our bodies.

'Take the case of my client, Mary. She was an office manager in her early 50s and described by her boss as the "back-bone" of the organisation. At her wit's end with the pain in her back, Mary was feeling increasingly guilty about taking so much time off. When she arrived at my office, it took her nearly five minutes to get out of the car – and under her smart suit, her spine was clearly twisted. She'd told me that she was prepared to "do whatever it takes" to get rid of the pain, which was growing in severity.

'After I'd explained to Mary about the strong connection between mind and body, and how our negative thoughts are often reflected in physical ill health, I'd gone on to tell her how the body sometimes uses physical symptoms to symbolise the message it's trying to tell us. Mary had then suggested that the physical body could perhaps be described as a barometer for what is going on in the mind! Pleased that she'd got the idea, I then asked her to tell me what she was "turning her back on."

'At first, she'd looked completely blank. As I'd gazed at her, an image of her arguing with a woman flashed into my mind. I asked her if there was any significance for her in what I'd imagined.

'"Oh yes," she said, "I've been arguing a lot with my daughter." She then went on to tell me how they'd hardly spoken for the last three years – and that when they did, they just ended up rowing. Mary's voice had started to sound a little whiny when she said that she felt she'd done so much for her daughter and that it had all been thrown back in her face. Mary described her feelings as "used, angry and hurt."

'I reminded Mary that as well as helping her daughter out, she'd also told me that she was seen as the "backbone" in her office too. I asked if perhaps her back was trying to tell her that she was doing too much for others, but not accepting any help or support for herself. At that, she'd begun to cry.

'I gently asked her to close her eyes and bring an image of her daughter to mind. Next, I encouraged her to express all her hurt and rage at her daughter in her imagination. Remember the subconscious mind doesn't distinguish between vivid imagination and reality.

'Once all the anger was out of her system, I asked her if she could make the decision to forgive her daughter. She nodded, so I then asked her to choose to accept and love her daughter for what she was, rather than condemn her for what she wasn't.

'It was simply amazing to watch. As Mary got to the end of the PEAR exercise, it was as though her face had visibly relaxed. She looked ten years younger! The final part of the exercise was for Mary to accept and love herself – and to ask for support from others when she needed it.

'But the really amazing thing only happened when we got to the end of the session together. When she stood up, her back was completely straight and her pain had gone!'

Pete, who up until this point had remained particularly quiet, raised his hand to ask a question. 'You're right, it really is some story. Like everyone else here, I'm really interested in what you're talking about. But how does all of this relate to our jobs – and business in general?'

It was a good point. And one that was often raised in my training programmes – usually on the first day!

'At the end of the day, success in business comes down to personal leadership. What this really means is that until we have self-mastery and excellent relationship skills, we've no real chance of creating lasting success. Yes, of course we may have the odd lucky break – but lucky breaks aren't repeatable, whereas personal leadership skills form the solid foundation on which all others skills can be built. Understanding people – and helping them achieve what they want in life – is the only way to create long term, sustainable success. Because we know ourselves better than anyone, it's often easier to start learning about what makes us tick and why we behave in the ways that we do before attempting to learn about other people. And, of course, once we have a greater understanding of ourselves, we can then apply what we know to other people and their situations. It's a great point Pete, and you'll have to trust me, but I think by the end of the programme tomorrow, it will all start to make a lot of sense.'

Pete smiled saying, 'No worries – I trust you!'

That was a great accolade, coming from a sceptic like Pete. Trust, as the del-egates would be learning the next day, is one of the key elements to creating great relationships. But for now we were looking at the mind/body connection and the dramatic effect that our memories and emotions can have. At the delegates' request, we explored the subject in a little more depth.

'When we had our session together', said Matt, 'it was really strange. You guys may remember that my hand always used to shake — well not any more!' He picked up his half-full coffee cup and showed the others how there were no longer any ripples on the liquid's surface. 'What was really odd was how she', Matt said, waving his head in my direction, 'spoke to the shakes! If I hadn't experienced it myself, I'd never have believed it.'

Before Matt could be asked what his 'shakes' had indeed represented, I took the helm again, hoping to avoid him the embarrassment of any further questions.

'Yes, it's amazing how the mind sometimes reveals repressed emotions through symbols. As Matt says, it all sounds pretty unbelievable but you'll see what I mean when I tell you Patricia's story!

'Pat was an accountant and we were only to have one session together. I think she'd rung me in desperation when her consultant had told her that she needed a potentially dangerous operation on her shoulder. As she'd walked through the door, she brought with her an air of immense sadness. I had the feeling that something traumatic had happened to her in the past. We talked a bit about the mind/body connection, and we laughed about how people who seem to have difficulty expressing themselves often go on to develop ailments around their throat — which of course is the area we associate with communication and free speech.

'Pat was pretty open-minded and she was up for letting me "talk" to her painful shoulder. I asked her — in her mind's eye — to travel into her shoulder

and describe what she could see. She replied that she could see a black pyramid with a lid. I then went on to ask her if it would be safe to remove the lid from the pyramid and when she nodded, I directed her to do so.

'Immediately she began to sob. It all came out, as though a dam had been lifted. Her father had both sexually and physically abused her as a little girl.

'After passing her a tissue, I asked her if she was prepared to do whatever was necessary to free her shoulder from pain. Again she nodded, and together we went through the PEAR exercise in which she eventually chose to forgive her father, while of course not condoning his actions. When we finished the exercise, I asked Pat to revisit the black pyramid. She seemed surprised by how much smaller it was.

'Her voice was barely a whisper. She told me that she'd never breathed a word to anyone about the abuse. The really sad thing is she thought that no one would believe her. After her twin daughters were born, Pat had pushed her worst nightmares aside, but now that they were growing older she was becoming increasingly worried about what their grandfather might do to them. She told me that she didn't want to tell them because she didn't want to shatter their image of him, and in order to protect them, she always ensured that she was present when he spent any time with the children.

'Suddenly the real message from Pat's shoulder became clear. She was "shouldering" the responsibility for both protecting her daughters and her father's reputation even though, of course, she didn't feel that he deserved it. But for all of her worrying about everyone else, she'd left herself out of the equation and now her mind was asking her – through her shoulder pain – to deal with the situation. We spoke about it for a while but she was absolutely adamant that she couldn't tell her daughters the horrible truth. To be honest, I knew that she had to be shocked into seeing the potential disaster that lay ahead if she kept quiet.

'I asked her how she'd feel if – for some reason – she wasn't there to protect her daughters and she later found out that they'd been abused by her father *in her absence. She'd know that she could have prevented the situation had she spoken up. A shocked silence greeted my words. Eventually, Pat acknowledged that I was right but felt that it would be very hard telling the truth after all this time. My heart went out to her. Over a cup of coffee, we worked together on a plan for telling her daughters in a way that would protect them but not frighten them.*

'When we finished, Pat left my office literally looking as though a weight had been lifted from her shoulders. A week later, she called to say that her shoulder pain had eased – and that she was sleeping better than she had for years. A further update a month later revealed that she had gently warned her daughters without going into too much detail – and that after her talk with them, her shoulder pain had gone entirely, which of course meant that she no longer needed an operation.'

'I find the whole thing just fascinating', piped up Matt, 'especially after our session together. And the great thing is that we can all use the PEAR process – which means that we have all the tools we need for healing ourselves!'

Points to ponder as you start to …

Be your own guru

1 Think about any ailments, aches or pains which you suffer from on a regular basis. Knowing that your body may be speaking meta-phorically to get your attention, what could its message be to you? Let your imagination play freely …

2 If you feel that your energy is blocked in some way, try 'talking' to the blockage. In your imagination, see what shape the blockage is, and what colour. When did it first arrive in your body? Can you simply visualise it getting smaller or vanishing all together – or is there someone or something that you need to deal with first on an emotional level?

3 Make a list of all the anger and hurt you're holding on to in con-nection with other people. Now add to the list all the things you're ashamed of having done. As you study your list, realise just how much negativity you're holding on to – and begin to see how much of an adverse effect it's having on your life.

4 Using your list, begin to apply the PEAR process. (It's best to do this exercise first in connection with a 'mini-trauma' in your life, so that you can get used to using the process. Only when you're comfortable with the PEAR process should you attempt to deal with the more deep and meaningful issues in your life. And of course, if you feel it's appropriate, you may want to see a fully qualified therapist. Being your own guru doesn't mean that you have to be an expert in all things, but you do have the choice in all things!)

In Section 4, you'll find some tools to help you on your way with the PEAR process.

Chapter 12
Using your body to read your mind

Through the science of kinesiology, we're able to see that there is a connection between mind, body and spirit. Kinesiology is based on muscle testing and enables us to communicate directly with the body. If something – whether it's a substance or thought – is good for you, your muscles are strengthened but if that 'something' is bad for you, then your muscles are weakened.

There's nothing to beat experiencing it for yourself. For this simple experiment, you'll need a partner, a glass of water and a bowl of sugar. First of all, you'll need to calibrate your natural strength. Stretch your right arm straight out to the side and ask your partner – just with two fingers – to push down on your arm while you at the same time push up. This isn't an exercise in 'super strength' – all you're both doing is exerting enough energy to be balanced.

Relax your arm and pick up the bowl of sugar and hold it with your left hand in front of your solar plexus (just below your rib cage). Now stretch out your right arm again and ask you partner to place his or her two fingers – with the same amount of force as he or she used the first time round – on your arm.

What did you observe?

Now try the same experiment, but this time replace the bowl of sugar with a glass of water.

What did you find this time?

Without wishing to prejudice your experiment, I'm pretty confident that I can predict the outcome. When you had the sugar in front of your solar plexus, your arm will have become weaker. This is because sugar is bad for you. When you did the second experiment with the glass of water, you're arm will have remained strong (if not stronger) because water is good for you. (Your body is made up of between 70–80% water, so it's something your body really needs to be replenished regularly. Most of us are dehydrated – which also has a detrimental effect on both our minds and bodies … but that's the stuff for different authors and different books!)

Using this form of muscle testing, we can easily see what is good for us and conversely, what doesn't serve us. But the really fascinating thing is that this phenomenon doesn't just work with tangible substances but also with our thoughts too.

By doing a similar experiment with both empowering and disempowering thoughts, it soon becomes very obvious that what we think about also has either a positive or negative effect on our bodies. Interestingly, the converse is also true. When we're suffering stress or pain within our bodies, it causes our thinking to become negative too – setting up a vicious downward spiral.

THE POWER OF THE PLACEBO ...

As a child, I remember asking my mother to explain the meaning of the term 'placebo'. She told me that it was a medical term, and that a placebo was a 'dummy' medication that looked like the real thing but which didn't have any real healing benefit.

'So what's the point of a placebo?', I asked.

She went on to explain that placebos were used in 'control' experiments to test the efficacy of a new drug. But the most amazing part of her explanation came when she told me that people taking a placebo often start to get better, simply because they believe that they are taking a real drug!

I was really impressed by the fact that the mind could produce a healing just through the power of belief. And I became really confused and disappointed when I asked her (in that annoying way that children do with their persistent 'why's') why more research wasn't being done into the power of the placebo? She'd simply smiled at me and said 'I'm afraid it just doesn't work that way!'

> **Guru Success Tip**
>
> If you want to be healthy and wealthy, harness the power of the placebo effect and make sure you think healthy and wealthy thoughts!

I dropped the conversation at that point but I was still fascinated by what she'd revealed. Years later I started reading books talking about the mind/body connection and was overjoyed to realise that my thoughts about the power of the placebo weren't misplaced after all!

HOW THE ANCIENT SHAMANS WEAVE THEIR MAGIC ...

Of course, when you stop to think about it, the power of the mind/body connection isn't new. The ancient medicine men, shamans and even witch doctors used the power of belief to bring about healing (or harm, depending on the intention) – which is why they were so good at bringing about healing in other people but less good at achieving it for themselves. Their understanding of the power of belief meant that many of the 'medicines' they used on others were little more than placebos in the traditional sense – and this knowledge rendered their concoctions useless for their own healing.

Of course, I'm not saying that all healers are snake oil merchants – far from it. Having trained in the eastern arts of energy healing, I can say quite categorically that they can have a remarkable impact. I've seen it happen time and time again. Once, when I was manning an exhibition stand promoting the beneficial effects of Reiki (a practice that involves the flow of Universal Energy through the practitioner's hands into the body of the recipient, to induce the relaxation response – which in turn brings about healing) a woman walked past, looking very angry. She turned to me and said that she'd just been stung by a wasp on her cheek and that she was really in pain.

'Would you like to try some Reiki for that?', I asked her.

'No', she replied, 'Well … what is it?'

After I'd explained, she looked at me as though I was mad. 'Well, whatever else', I offered, 'why don't you just come and sit in my comfortable chair for a few minutes – that way you can get over the shock.'

'OK, thank you', she replied, adding a moment later, 'and if you want to do some Reiki – whatever it is – feel free!'

Smiling at how she'd already begun to change her tune, I sat her down and placed my hands a couple of inches away from the side of her face. Immediately, my hands felt very hot and within a quarter of an hour my 'client' suddenly burst into floods of tears. Passing her a tissue, I carried on with what I was doing and it wasn't long before her tears subsided. My hands started to feel cooler and I continued the treatment for another five minutes. Just before I finished, she suddenly got up out of the chair and looked me deep in the eyes saying, 'I don't know what you've done but I feel completely different. I'm no longer in pain with the wasp sting and I feel as though I've had a couple of hours sleep – amazing!' As I looked at her, I was surprised at just how much better she seemed, it was as though she'd dropped a lot of tension from her face – and I suspected that her sudden outburst of tears had had something to do with it. I really knew something profound had happened when the woman's companions came back past the stand an hour or so later, saying that they just couldn't believe the change in their friend!

It's not so much a case of mind over matter – it's more that mind and matter are intertwined. A girl – Tina – on a training course once told me that she'd developed a horrible headache and that the tablets she'd taken hadn't made any difference. I decided to try something new but while I knew it was an experiment, I knew that she had to believe that what we were about to do would definitely work.

> **Guru Success Tip**
>
> Powerful beliefs can heal as well harm. Becoming consciously aware about your negative beliefs and how they're harming you is vital when you're on the path to being your own guru!

I stretched my arm out in front of me, with my palm facing forwards – as though I was wanting to stop traffic. Then I asked her – in her mind's eye only – to imagine that she could connect the pain in her head with a taut energy line (like an umbilical cord) to my outstretched hand. When she nodded, I suggested that we should see whether we could move the pain half an inch by me moving my hand, which would in turn tug on the energy line which was attached to her pain.

'Yes! It's moved, I can do it! The pain's moved!'

'Excellent', I replied. 'Just as I expected; I knew you'd be good at this. So, if we can move it half an inch let's try moving it again, this time by an inch.'

Seeing that this too had worked, I continued moving the pain in this way – taking it all the way down her left arm and out through her fingertips. I'm not sure which one of us was more surprised by the turn of events – but it proved to me yet again that if we believe in something strongly enough, we can make it our reality.

HOW SYMBOLISM HAS A PART TO PLAY …

Our subconscious minds – particularly when they don't want to deal with something traumatic – often use symbols to get our attention. Sometimes we receive a mental flash of something unusual or occasionally we see something in the external world that seems to register within us as being particularly significant.

Amusingly, this happened to a friend when he was looking to adopt a new approach towards a problem with a work colleague. For a while my friend had felt that he was in a stalemate situation but when he parked his car one morning before going to work, he saw on the payment station under 'pay here' the immortal words: 'change is possible'! He burst out laughing – much to the bewilderment of passers-by – and decided to approach the situation with his work colleague from a new angle. And this time it worked – and the stalemate was broken.

Our bodies are an excellent guidance system – particularly for people suffering with chronic illnesses and ailments. Curiously, the body tends to speak in puns – or at least reflect our colloquial language. Remember my friend who talked about 'people being a pain in neck' – and who's now suffering from osteoporosis in her neck?

Often the symbolism is a little odd, to say the least. When I was studying a new form of healing therapy which involved the use of symbols, we were asked to work in pairs – and see what symbolic images came to mind for our partner. I was appalled when the only image I got was a jar of marmalade! I felt far too embarrassed to say this to the person I was working with and kept ignoring the image, even though it wouldn't go away. In the end I couldn't think of anything else but this jar of marmalade – and the teacher, knowing that I had something, persuaded me to speak up.

Eventually, I said in a small voice, 'What would a jar of marmalade mean to you?'

I'd been expecting derision, but instead my partner replied, 'Wow, yes, that would mean to me that life was pretty sweet but with bitter elements to it.' Stunned by her interpretation, I then went on to ask her about the bitter elements in her life. It wasn't long before we used the PEAR process – and the feedback I got from her was most encouraging!

Similarly, in one session I found myself working with a client who seemed to have an energetic barrier around him. He was clearly a great guy, but it was hard to warm to him or feel any sense of connection. I sensed coldness around him – and asked – knowing he was having significant problems in his marriage – whether he felt this might be cutting him off in his relationships. He nodded and, in response, I likened his situation to living in an igloo! 'It's as though you're living on the inside, cut off from the warmth of all the people on the outside.' Again he nodded – and sniffed. It felt like we were making progress.

> **Guru Success Tip**
>
> Understand that your imagination is the best place to begin any new enterprise – whether it's your personal healing or an entre-preneurial business opportunity!

How to lose the igloo? I suggested that my client light a candle and use the heat to slowly melt the igloo – and that as the igloo melted away, he'd be able to see his family and friends waiting for him – where they'd always been – on the outside. (Time, space and practicality are thankfully not considerations that have to be taken into account in the imagination !) As he began to melt the igloo in his imagination, he started to smile as he saw that his family and friends really were there!

While this may seem like nothing more than a trick of the mind, the point is that a real healing took place. Who cares how it happened? I caught up with my client a couple of years later and he told me that his marriage was now better than ever and that he'd managed to become the envy of his colleagues as he was achieving not only financial success but was also managing to create a perfect work/life balance.

Whether we're aware of it or not, all of us have the ability to pick up on the feelings of those around us. Whether people are happy or sad, angry or depressed, we're aware at an energy level of their feelings. If we're not consciously aware though, we can end up adopting other people's feelings and making them our own. Now this isn't a problem if you're surrounded by happy, healthy people – but spend too long in the company of negative people and you'll soon start feeling down yourself.

Finally, when I'm taking someone through the PEAR exercise, I often ask them to imagine that the other person has a gift for them. It's amazing how beneficial this can be! Often clients receive a bunch of flowers, a book, or something that's personally meaningful. I also ask the person to think about what gift they'd give – and in this way the healing process is often completed.

Chapter 13
Learning to talk the talk

*I*t was early afternoon – and I knew from the animated discussions that had been taking place around the lunch table that the delegates were already starting to apply what they'd learned from the morning session to their own situations. Laughter had regularly punctuated the conversation and it appeared to me that the group were really starting to bond – a feeling that was to be later echoed by the delegates themselves. But I was really pleased when Pete had said 'Right everyone, we've finished lunch – let's get back to the room, so that the afternoon mind stretching can begin!'

Traditionally, after lunch is known as the 'graveyard slot' – with much of their energy being diverted to digesting their food, people's concentration levels tend to dip. Sometimes, I use this phenomenon to my advantage by conducting a guided visualisation exercise but sensing the upbeat mood of the delegates, I chose to focus instead on the power of language.

After they'd all taken their seats, I asked for a volunteer. Not knowing what was coming next, everyone sat back – hoping that perhaps one of their colleagues would accept the challenge. 'It's always good to volunteer early on',

I laughed, 'because the likelihood is that what you'll be asked to volunteer for later will be far more difficult!'

At that, Pete's hand immediately shot up. 'In that case, choose me!'

Inviting Pete to step up to the front, I stood next to him. 'How are your acting skills?' I asked him. 'Not bad', he replied, frowning slightly at the oddity of the question. 'Actually, I was in a couple of school plays – will that help?'

*'Absolutely', I replied. Turning my attention back to include the rest of the delegates, I asked if anyone had heard of kinesiology. As they all shook their heads, I continued, 'Kinesiology is, in a way, the science behind the mind/body connection. Basically, it's about using muscle testing to identify energy blockages in the body. Often kinesiology is used for testing whether a particular substance – be it food, drink, vitamin supplements or even tobacco – is beneficial or harmful to an individual. However, today we're going to be using it in connection with language, in particular the "self-talk" that we're all playing in our heads all the time. You know that little voice? It's the one that gives us a running commentary on life, making things fit according to our beliefs, rather than reality. Well, Pete is going to demonstrate for us exactly how this little voice **really** affects us.'*

First of all, we needed to calibrate Pete's natural strength. Having checked which was his dominant hand, I asked Pete to raise his right arm out to the side. I placed two fingers on his wrist and instructed him to push up while I pushed down. 'It's not about seeing how strong you are, it's more a case of both of us knowing how much pressure we need to exert in order to be in a state of equilibrium.

'Great, now relax. Bring your arm down to your side again, while I explain what we'll be doing next', I instructed him. 'In a moment, I'm going to be asking you to demonstrate, for all the people here, how it is to be really depressed. How would you stand?'

Pete took on an exaggerated stance of someone who was really experiencing the blues. His shoulders sagged, his knees buckled slightly and his chin started curling in towards his neck, as he kept his eyes firmly fixed on the floor. The others started to laugh, partly because of Pete's exemplary acting skills, but also partly out of embarrassment. While I wanted everyone to enjoy the demonstration, I also wanted Pete to be completely focused on the job in hand, so I brought my straight index finger up in front of my mouth in a gesture that made it very clear that I wanted silence.

'Good, you're doing really well. Feel that sense of heaviness, of depression – and remember, you're here to instruct the rest of the class in how it is to be depressed. It's like a method acting lesson for them. Now, in a moment, I'm going to ask you to repeat, just five times, "I'm weak, I'm worthless, I'm useless."'

Pete looked at me with anxiety written all over his face. 'Don't worry', I reassured him, 'I won't leave you in that state, I promise!'

He was already doing a great job. I could feel Pete's energy sinking. 'I'm weak, I'm worthless, I'm useless', I prompted him. Pete started saying the words, getting quieter with each repetition. He really did look and sound desperately unhappy. As soon as he'd said the words for the final time, I asked him to raise his right arm again, and to push up while at the same time, I placed my two fingers on his arm, just as I had on the previous occasion. But this time, it was as though Pete had no internal strength and my two fingers pushed his arm straight back down to his side.

'How do you feel Pete?'

'Weak, worthless and useless!' he replied with a small, nervous laugh.

'And how do the rest of you feel, watching Pete?' I asked the others.

'I feel terrible', said Jenny immediately. 'I feel weak, worthless and useless with him. Part of me wants to sort him out – and the other part wants to run a mile!'

'Great observation', I replied. 'It's odd, I know where this exercise is going – I do it often enough – but every time I run through it with someone, I can feel my own energy just evaporating too! And while Pete was repeating "I'm weak, I'm worthless, I'm useless," it was fascinating to look at all of you. It was as though none of you could bear to look at Pete. Most of you were either staring down at the table or fiddling with something. It was as though there was a deep, almost primeval urge to disassociate from someone expressing such negativity.'

'You're so right', chimed in Jenny again. 'When people around me feel down, it's as though it's catching. I think I'm really affected by how people are around me, which is why I suppose you said earlier that we should be careful to spend our time with positive people!'

'Absolutely', I replied, 'and worse, what effect do you – not just you, Jenny but everyone here – what effect do you have on the people around us when you're feeling down and bad about life?'

Initially silence greeted my question. Then they all began to speak at once. Matt's voice was the loudest and everyone soon stopped to listen to what he had to say. 'It's as though everything has just become clear to me in the last couple of minutes. When I'm feeling down, it's as though everything starts going wrong – but maybe it's me that's causing it to happen! I suppose that other people are picking up on my negativity, which is causing them to be awkward too, without either them or me realising it. It has awful implications for when we're out there selling doesn't it?' Matt asked his colleagues, looking around the table for confirmation from them.

Judging by the number of nods that greeted his remark, Matt's observation had clearly struck home. Throughout the discussion, Pete had remained standing in his 'I'm really depressed' stance and quietly he touched me on the arm saying, 'You promised not to leave me in this state! I feel terrible, probably because in order to do the exercise, I decided to tap into how I felt when my father died last year. I don't want to carry on feeling like this. Make it stop!'

'Of course, Pete', I replied, gently putting my hand on his shoulder. 'But what a great observation you've just made. Isn't is amazing that how you are physically – how you stand, where you look, what you say, affects how you **feel** and *vice versa. By taking more conscious control over our physical bodies, we can alter how we feel – and as you now know from this morning's work, how you feel affects how you behave, and of course how you behave dictates what happens to you in life. Having just said that, I can now really understand what it means to be a co-creator in life! I've understood the term intellectually before, but until this moment I've never quite got it, so thank you Pete.'*

Once again, I'd been reminded that these sessions always taught me something new too …

'Right Pete', I said, turning my full attention to him. 'Now what you're going to do is imagine that we've hired an enormous stadium and that it's full of people who've heard about you – and what you teach about being positive. They've all come here today to hear what you have to say. They want – they need – to learn from you. So, if you were to teach this huge crowd to be really positive and powerful, how would you stand?'

Immediately, Pete's posture changed. Ramrod straight, he planted his feet about a foot apart, raised his chin so that he could easily look right to the back of the room and brought his hands up in front of his chest, clenching his fists in an attitude of power.

While the others may not have been consciously aware of it yet, the energy in the room seemed to shift immediately. All the delegates began to wriggle around in their chairs, straightening their backs and fixing their focus firmly on Pete. Already, there was an intense rapport between them all. When one of their number felt bad, they all felt bad. But as soon as one of them started to feel good and act supremely confident, it was as though a switch had been flicked. Clearly, the 'feeling great' state was just as contagious as the 'feeling bad' one. Unconsciously, all the delegates began to mirror Pete's behaviour, not least because at this point, he'd acquired a temporary leadership position simply by being the one standing at the front doing the demonstration.

'Fantastic', I continued. 'Now, I want you to say, with as much feeling as possible, the following sentence five times. "I am strong, I am powerful, I am magnificent!"'

Bursts of laughter had broken out around the room when I'd said the word 'magnificent'. *

In order to encourage him, I started to say the words with him, emphasising the words and reinforcing them with my body language. Pete soon got the hang of it and he became more convincing with each repetition. When he said the words the final time, his voice was filled with tremendous power and determination and his body language was invincible.

'I AM STRONG, I AM POWERFUL, I AM MAGNIFICENT!!' boomed Pete's voice. As he finished, the rest of the delegates broke into spontaneous applause. The atmosphere in the room had changed remarkably, a fact noticed by Matt.

'That's incredible. No, not just your performance Pete – although that was indeed pretty amazing! For me what's really incredible is that we've all completely changed how we feel in the space of less than 15 minutes! It seems impossible now to remember how uncomfortable it felt watching Pete grapple with being depressed. Presumably, we can all have that much affect – either positively or negatively – on other people?'

I nodded in response to his question. 'You're absolutely right, Matt. But as you'll see tomorrow, it's when we're able to get in rapport with someone that the magic really starts to happen.'

'Roll on tomorrow', said Matt laughingly.

'Patience', I replied, 'we've still got lots of amazing stuff to get through today! And before we move on, I want you to consider that Pete repeated the words only five times – but in reality how often do we repeat the same negative things to ourselves over and over again?'

---

* Curiously, the word 'magnificent' seems to have that effect on many of the groups I work with. I like to believe it's because we're not brought up to recognise our magnificence, but my delightful commissioning editor John assures me it's because the term 'magnificent' is something of a double entendre!

Points to ponder as you start to ...
Be your own guru

1 For the next week, make the effort to become more consciously aware of your own self-talk. Is that little voice programming you positively or negatively? You may want to set an alarm on your watch or mobile phone to go off at regular intervals – and when it does, track back over what that little voice has been telling you, you may be surprised!

2 Take some time out and think about your life 'stories' – they're the ones that you tend to share with someone new at the earliest opportunity! Do you constantly replay the 'poor me' story, sounding like a stuck record? Who or what are the things you blame in your life?

3 What judgements and criticisms do you regularly hear from your inner critic? With whom did those messages first originate? Consider using the PEAR process to set yourself free. How is your life enhanced – or what do you need to let go of – in order to change your story to a more positive one?

4 Think about your language patterns. Are they positive and is your language focused on what you want? Or are you unwittingly giving power to what you don't want, purely because of the words you use?

5 Make a mental note to become more aware of how you programme other people. They say that parents and teachers make the best hypnotists! Are you programming the people around you to feel positive, encouraged and good about themselves? Or could time spent with you be programming them for lifelong misery?

Chapter 14
Watch your language

Frightened of being carted off to the funny farm, we may not care to admit it, but we're all hearing voices in our heads, all the time! Well, to be more precise, we're listening to our *own* inner voice all the time. Worse, there's no getting away from that inner voice – or at least there isn't until you learn to meditate, at which point you'll be able to switch off the internal mental chatter for short periods of time.

The mental chatter is a sign that we're living in a state of duality, our normal state of being. From this perspective we see ourselves as separate from other people and indeed the rest of the world 'out there'. We experience duality when we're operating from our ego, which for most of us is most of the time! The ego, as we'll be seeing shortly, is the root cause of a lot of our misery – but viewed in the right light, it can go on to be our salvation.

But for now let's focus on the power of our internal self-talk. Whether we indulge in positive or negative thinking, at the end of the day it's our choice. But we can only make that choice when we're consciously aware of our thoughts. Most of the time, we're operating on the subconscious mind's default system, which as we've already seen, tends to compare current experiences with those from the past. The ego loves to indulge in judging and comparing and if we didn't have positive experiences when we were younger, then the chances are that we'll view ourselves as 'not being good enough'. Add to that the voices of our parents and teachers and it's no wonder so many of us are striving to win approval. And it's not necessarily other people's approval that we crave but our own!

The voice in our head then, tends to focus on self-criticism. This can work to some extent in our favour – at least in terms of fulfilling our ambitions and goals – as that still, small voice of conscience demands that we don't rest on our laurels. However, fulfilling our ambitions isn't the same as feeling fulfilled – or even happy! If we're to achieve a degree of self-appreciation, we can only achieve it by being consciously aware of the little voice in our head and then questioning the truth of what it's actually saying.

Guru Success Tip

Be careful that when you're being overawed by other people's success stories that you're not just buying into their 'personal press releases'!

As a former journalist who later went into public relations for a couple of years, I found myself writing press releases for other people's businesses. By the time I'd finished hand-crafting a story fit for the newspapers I realised that, while I hadn't actually lied in what I'd written, I'd been very careful to give the story a glossy spin. It's what the clients were paying for! The problem is that – especially now that we're all so busy – most of us take in what we read or hear at face value, without questioning how much spin has been involved.

Years later, it began to dawn on me that in the stories we run internally about ourselves and other people, we're also effectively writing our own press releases and believing our own spin! And it's not just the stories about ourselves and what's happening to us that we give this treatment to – we also apply it to what we believe to be true about other people and outside events. Prejudice and intolerance only arise because of our 'inner critic' – which judges, compares and decides what is right and wrong against its own criteria. But these criteria are not based in truth – they're based on *our* beliefs and experiences! And the more we listen to the negative inner voice, the more we believe that what it has to say is true! This can cause havoc, as one of my clients, Simon, had already found out to his cost …

When I first met Simon, he admitted that he'd always been an under-achiever and something of a procrastinator, getting into trouble for missing deadlines – a fact that particularly irritated his colleagues. I asked him when this behaviour had started – and he replied that he just attributed it to being a part of his personality. With deeper questioning, Simon admitted to feeling an inappropriate fear of authority figures – citing one time when he suffered sleepless nights after a manager had expressed disappointment in him and uncertainty over his future.

Guru Success Tip

Impress your colleagues by making sure that you 'under promise but over deliver'!

Simon had an endearing personality and this, coupled with his overwhelming need to please people, had resulted in his trying to take on too many projects at work. He was having to confront the fact that not only was his work suffering, but now so was his health. He realised that something needed to change – and drastically – but he had no idea how to help himself. As I sat with him, I idly began to wonder what Simon would have been like as a child. What came to mind was an image of a little boy, wearing a dishevelled school uniform, carrying a limp teddy bear in his hand. In my imagination, he didn't look like a happy little boy at all. Not wanting to pre-empt his thinking, I asked him about his childhood – and whether or not he'd enjoyed school.

Shaking his head vehemently, Simon replied that he'd hated his school-days – and indeed didn't like thinking about his childhood at all. With a tight smile, he told me about his memories of being humiliated by a teacher in junior school – who'd accused him of cheating. In fact, his friend had been copying Simon's work – but when the teacher found out, he said nothing – he didn't even apologise!

Even though he'd been only seven years old at the time, the memory of that humiliation had remained with him throughout his life. Before I could say anything further, Simon's face turned white and then, as the tears finally started to flow, a blotchy red. Pulling a handkerchief from his pocket, Simon spilled the sorry tale of how he'd been mercilessly taunted at school by five bullies who resented his prowess on the sports field. When he tried to stand up to his tormentors on a couple of occasions, he soon realised that the odds were stacked against him. Instead, he'd taken evasive action and had given up sport at school. As a child he'd learned that success equated with pain, and his inner talk was focused on keeping him small and unsuccessful, so that he wouldn't ever again suffer being unpopular.

Avoiding conflict consequently became a survival mechanism for Simon, who resorted to the same tactic in his adult life. His fear of conflict kept him in the lower rungs of management – a source of frustration to his family who'd always believed that he was destined for much greater things.

Acknowledging the cause of his difficulties was the first step. Next, I took Simon through the PEAR process. By forgiving his adversaries, he resolved the conflict within his mind. At last, the inner voice which had kept goading him was silenced. No longer was he hearing his inner voice telling him that 'being successful only causes trouble'. Free from the patterns of the past, Simon was able to rewrite his future.

AND THE INNER VOICE ISN'T THE ONLY DANGER …

As we've already seen, the subconscious works to bring what we focus on into reality – and this applies to the language we use too. Using self-language effectively means that we programme ourselves for success. Sadly, the converse is also true.

It's important to remember that the subconscious tends to take things literally – almost in a childlike fashion. It makes sense therefore, to ensure that any instructions we issue to it are crystal clear. For example, have you ever tried to get fitter? I'll bet you a pound to a dollar that your attempts failed. How do I know? Well, your subconscious mind simply won't have understood the 'try' instruction. This isn't always a concept that's easy to explain, as Lynda, a delegate on one of my courses a while back, discovered …

'This isn't making any sense to me', said Lynda, who was having problems getting her head around the whole concept of self-language. 'Why will I fail if I *try* to do something?' The rest of that particular training group looked confused too, so I invited them all to stand behind their chairs and await my instruction.

'Right, listen carefully, because I'm going to say this only once. I want you to try to pick up your chair.'

Several people looked confused and one young man immediately started to pick up the chair, waving it gracefully around in the air.

'No!' I barked in what I hoped was a school-mistressy tone. 'I did NOT say pick up the chair. I asked you to TRY to pick up the chair!'

Confusion reigned. They all started looking at one another. What was it that I really wanted them to do? 'Confused?' I asked the group. 'Of course you are', I continued. 'After all, you can either pick up the chair or not pick up the chair. There isn't a halfway point. Telling you to "try" didn't make any sense – and every time you tell your subconscious mind that you're going to try it doesn't understand the command either! Worse, if you say you're going to try, your subconscious mind knows that deep down, you're not really committed. For example, have you ever asked someone to do something for you, only to have them respond to you that they'll try? In your heart of hearts, you know that whatever you've asked them to do probably isn't going to get done!'

Comprehension dawned on the faces of the group. Lynda was the first to speak. 'Well', she said, 'that's a lot clearer now. I guess after that, I know why I've never succeeded when I've tried to lose weight!'

> **Guru Success Tip!**
>
> Always commit to do something – knowing that if you set out only to try, the probability is that you'll fail!

And talking of losing weight … What's the first thing you do when you lose your car keys? You look for them! The subconscious mind wants to keep you safe and it associates the concept of 'loss' with being 'bad for you'. It will therefore do all it can to avoid you having to experience loss. And in our weight-loss scenario, the subconscious will avoid loss by making you feel hungrier – filling your mind with the thought of doughnuts, or whatever you have a particular susceptibility for. The result? You put on weight – and continue to wonder why losing weight is so difficult!

Getting around this isn't hard, once you know how. The trick is to colour your language with a positive slant. So, 'I want to lose weight' becomes 'I want to be slim.' But even here, there's a hidden snare. The statement isn't quite right yet because your subconscious will now do its very best to ensure that you're kept in a state of 'wanting'! The ideal statement would be something along the lines of, 'Starting right now, I'm doing everything I can to be my ideal weight'.

This sounds as though it's bordering on an affirmation and while it's pretty close, there's a distinction. Being clear in what you articulate to your subconscious is a 'commitment of intention', while an affirmation tends to work on the idea that 'if I say it often enough, it'll come true!' While there is more than a grain of truth in that, I have a slight problem with affirmations because they seem to be almost confirming an untruth – simply by you saying them. To put it another way, you don't (unless you really do deserve that place at the funny farm) tend to look in the mirror and shout, 'I'M A HUMAN BEING, I'M A HUMAN BEING!' The reason you don't do this is because you know it to be so and therefore you take it for granted. I suspect that when you repeat affirmations that you don't *quite* believe, your subconscious mind takes it with a large grain of salt, thus sabotaging your best efforts.

I've often wondered whether the Mediterranean people are happier than the rest of us – not only because of their sunshine, fabulous food and glorious wines – but also because of their language. Does this sound far-fetched? Well, not when you start to consider that while we say, for example, 'I *am* hungry', or 'I *am* frightened', or 'I *am* cold', in French, Spanish or Italian this translates into 'I *have* anger', 'I *have* fear' or 'I *have* cold'. Somehow, with these latter language patterns, there is a distancing between the person and the experience, while in English, it's as though we're saying that what we feel *is* us!

And finally, learn from the mistake my farmer friend was determined to repeat each year. Every winter, he used to say, 'I don't know why it is, but every Christmas I get a cold!' No matter how often I suggested that he was programming himself he'd take no notice. It was as though his subconscious mind was saying, 'Well, there's no need ... but if you want this misery, I can make it happen!' The only beneficiary in this scenario was the local purveyor of flu remedies ...

Chapter 15

Death is our teacher

I took a deep breath and began to speak. *'It was March 2002 and I knew that in two days time, I was going to die ...'*

I already had the delegates' attention. Pausing a little for dramatic effect, I continued, 'I'd woken with a start and the sweat had already made my scalp damp. It was a hot and sticky night in a chic hotel in one of Thailand's most stunning resorts. We were due to leave for home in just two days – and at that moment, in the middle of the night, I had an intuitive knowing that our plane was going to crash. Although my (former) husband was snoring gently next to me, I was alone with my terror.

'We'd already argued during the holiday', I continued. 'A plane had crashed that week in nearby Taiwan – and we were due to fly with the same airline! My husband was a "news junkie" and, as a result, I'd been fed on a relentless diet of TV news reports that described – in great detail – the airline's very poor safety record. I wanted to switch flights but my ever-pragmatic husband told me not to be so ridiculous – we'd paid for the tickets and that was that. Over the next few days, I buried my anxiety, hoping that he was

*right and I was wrong. But when I woke up that unforgettable night in such a deep state of panic, I knew I'd been wrong to ignore my premonition. I was also deeply angry – not at my husband – but at me. Why hadn't I stood up for myself? Why hadn't I **demanded** that we change airlines? Why had I given my power away, yet again?'*

The room was silent. Jenny was sitting with her chin in her hands, drinking in my every word.

Picking up the story again, I carried on, 'As I lay there in silent dread, the tears began to flow. My eyes strained to see the luminous hands on the digital clock, but without my contact lenses everything was a blur. From nowhere came a silent invitation to focus on my breathing and as I did so, gently becoming aware of nothing more than my in-breath, followed by my out-breath, my pounding heart had begun to slow. I started to feel calmer – serene even. So what if I was going to die? Why was I crying? Did it really matter to the world whether I lived or died?'

Looking around the room, I added, 'We've all been to funerals – and you know that you've no choice but to pick up the pieces and get on with living – however close you were to the person who's died.

'My own belief is that our "essence" – or soul if you prefer – lives on after our body dies, and that belief has got stronger from the past life regression sessions that I've done with a wide variety of clients. What didn't make sense to me was why, if I knew my soul was eternal, had I been in such a fear-ful state in that hotel room? Slowly, it began to dawn on me. My life was completely devoid of meaning.

*'Looking at it later in the cold light of day, that was probably a bit of an exaggeration but in the black of the night, it seemed that all those things I'd struggled with – building up a business, two marriages, difficulties in close family relationships, my towering in-tray, my low self-esteem – were point-less in the great scheme of things. My death would be but a blip in everyone else's life experience. To be honest, I wanted to **matter** more. The ghastly*

truth was that my ego was traumatised by the thought that everyone I knew would be able to get on with their lives perfectly well without me!'

A chuckle caught in Pete's throat. He'd been accused in the past of being stubborn and ego-centric and it seemed that my lesson was hitting home for him too!

'We can only be fully alive "in the moment"', I said, taking time to look at each of the delegates in turn. I snapped my fingers loudly to illustrate my point, explaining, 'The past and future don't actually exist. The moment when I clicked my fingers has already gone for ever. None of us can ever get that moment back. What we imagine being true about tomorrow isn't as yet a reality either. That night, I came to see just how much time I'd wasted in the "dead zone" – feeling angry at what had happened in the past and fearing what lay ahead in my future! I asked myself how often I'd really been "alive in the now?"'

As I paused again Jenny said quietly. 'As you're speaking, I'm beginning to see that much of my time and energy is spent trying to create security. But what you're really saying is that security is nothing really but an illusion.'

*'Absolutely', I replied, nodding at her. 'But the security we crave isn't so much physical security, but **emotional** security. And without that emotional security, none of us is ever in a position to realise our full potential. Up until that night, much of my previous understanding about life had been merely intellectual but then, facing the reality of my own imminent death, I'd been forced not only to feel the emotion of abject fear but also to square up to it!'*

After taking a sip of water, I started speaking again, 'The whole experience had only taken a couple of hours but I knew I'd undergone a major "shift" in perception. Once I'd transcended my deepest fear, my terror had lifted and been replaced with a sense of peace. I could see that it's only when we have faced ourselves – and our annihilation – that we stand any chance of finding freedom from the emotional and psychic ties that bind us. It wasn't long before another intuitive flash hit me. This time, I knew that the plane I was due to fly back home on had never been going to crash at all – but that I'd been given the terrifying experience as an invitation from my soul to review my life and make the changes that would enable me to follow my spiritual purpose. It was as though I had a stark choice: ignore the message and be given a more serious (probably) health-oriented wake up call in the future – or listen to my soul's whisperings and simply dismantle the life I'd taken so much trouble to create! Some choice, huh?!'

'Yeah, I can see how the experience was something of a wake-up call', said Pete. 'But you don't strike me as someone who's living a really debauched life! I've not seen you outside with the smokers during the breaks and you don't strike me as a heavy drinker either – so what were the changes that your soul was asking you to make?'

As he'd spoken, Pete had put a slight emphasis on the word 'soul' – making me feel that perhaps I was taking him and his colleagues a little too far out of their comfort zone. I began wondering whether to water down my words – but I felt that patronising them in this way would be grossly insulting. Wondering what to say next, Pete unwittingly came to my rescue by repeating his question, 'Go on, what was it your soul wanted you to hear?'

'Well Pete, I may not smoke or drink much – but I did have one addiction. And it's an addiction that's haunted me throughout my life. It was an addiction to other people's approval. All my life I'd had an overwhelming need to do whatever I could to avoid rejection and criticism. That night, I began to think about all my relationships. As a believer in the healing power of unconditional love, I've taught about forgiveness and compassion for years – and have plenty of first-hand experiences to demonstrate its effectiveness. But somehow this night was different. It was as though my soul was calling me to forgive everyone who had ever hurt me – including myself! And although it was exceedingly uncomfortable, I also chose to explore how I'd hurt others too. Needless to say, it was an experience that left me squirming. When we're emotionally scarred – and we all are to some extent – we tend to perpetuate the hurt by wounding others, even if we're not aware of it.

'I felt drawn to let go of every single attachment to everyone and everything in my life. It was as though I was being invited to remain connected but unattached. Looking at my life through the microscope in this way helped me see just how ridiculous my need for security and other people's approval really was. If my death wasn't going to have great repercussions around the world, or even with people I considered to be close, then why had I been setting such store by other people's acceptance of me? I also recognised that I needed to make a pact with myself to live the rest of my life in truth. I no longer had the right to pretend to be anything other than who I am. And, as I was to discover, "coming out" – whether it's in terms of sexuality or spirituality – isn't always easy!'

I went on to tell the delegates how, for years, I'd wanted to change career and move out of journalism and into the world of personal development but hadn't done so because I simply hadn't had the courage. Apart from having the responsibilities of owning and editing two business magazines, I'd been cowardly and ducked out of following my heart, mainly because I feared that people would laugh at my aspirations. But, as time went on, I found that merely studying a variety of western and eastern therapeutic techniques on the quiet wasn't enough and I knew I was being prodded to come clean about my intuitive abilities. I realised that I faced ridicule from those around me – especially my close family – but as my perspective was beginning to shift, I felt I could now (pretty!) comfortably survive any derision.

Finishing off the story, I said, 'I knew that my destiny lay on a different path – and that it was now time for me to stick my head above the parapet. I was scared and yet strangely exhilarated! Once I got home and started dismantling life as I'd known it, really surreal things started happening. As well as amazing opportunities and synchronicities, I started meeting new people – and often we'd feel an instantaneous and deep soul connection. I began to feel better than I had in a long time and other people commented on how well – and even more strangely, how different – I looked.'

'Wow, what an amazing experience', one of the younger women on the course exclaimed. 'But you never told us about your plane. Did it crash?'

Pete and Matt both snorted with laughter, with the latter adding, 'Of course the plane didn't crash … how would she be here to tell her story if the plane had crashed?!'

As the laughter died down, I told the delegates that they were now going to be taking part in their own soul journey.

Inviting them to lie down on the floor and to make themselves comfortable, I explained that for the following half an hour or so, they'd get to experience the power of guided visualisation for themselves. 'You'll probably get lots of personal insights, so make sure that you have a paper and pen handy for as soon as it's over!'

I talked the delegates down into a state of deep relaxation and then, very gently, began to take them on a journey to their own funeral.

'You decide to fast forward the movie that is your life, and easily find the point – in many years' time – in which your funeral is taking place. Much to your relief and joy, you begin to realise that your funeral doesn't signify the end of "you," but only the body that you have known in this lifetime. It's as though you realise, maybe for the first time, that your essence is eternal', I guided, continuing, 'as you float among the mourners at your funeral, you're aware that you can see and hear what's going on. It's as though you're really there but with one difference: no one else is aware of your presence.

'You look around – how many people have come? Are you disappointed with the turnout, or surprised by just how many people there are in attendance? You see members of your family and your close friends and begin to really feel their emotions. You find yourself able to listen in on their conversations. Are they saying that yours was a life well-lived? Are they full of admiration for you because you made the most of every precious moment – or are they saying it was a shame you constrained yourself out of fear?

'You watch as someone stands up and walks to the front to deliver the eulogy. Who is speaking and what do they say? Do they talk about your warmth, humour and vitality – or are the gathered mourners just treated to a list of your scholastic, professional and perhaps sporting accomplishments?

'As you listen, do you feel that your life has been exciting and colourful or "correct" and colourless?

'You notice on one of the seats that someone has folded a newspaper page to reveal your obituary. You begin to read it – what does it say? What would you have liked it to say? If you had the chance to write your obituary, how would it read? You smile inwardly as you remember the remark that, on their deathbeds, nobody ever says that they wished they'd attended more meetings! You begin to remember the things in life that brought you great joy – together with the things in life that you worried about, but which never happened. If you were to be given a second chance to do things differently, what would you change? What would you do more of – and what time wasting things would you eliminate?'

I allowed the delegates to remain in contemplation for several minutes and then gently talked them back into waking reality. As they were writing about what they'd learned on their soul journey, I began to think about what was coming next on our mutual odyssey of self-discovery. I wondered just what they'd make of the suggestion that perhaps they were nothing more than a figment of their imagination …

Points to ponder as you start to ...
Be your own guru

1 Take some time out and think about your life – how would your obituary read if it was written today? Does this satisfy you? If you could write your future obituary, what would it say?

2 Take a trip on the soul journey for yourself; to make it easier, you'll find a script at the back of the book.

3 Make a list of all the things you do in your everyday life. Write an 'F' by the items that make you fulfilled and a 'T' by the items that make you feel trapped. Write down the following question: How can I do *less* of the things marked with a 'T'? Now write at least 20 suggestions. (By writing this – and making yourself come up with at least 20 suggestions – you're accessing the creative part of your brain!) Now do the same exercise with the question, 'How can I do *more* of the things marked with an "F"?'

4 If you could wave a magic wand – and you absolutely knew that failure wasn't a possibility, how would your life look?

5 Think about the limitations in your life. Have you been blaming 'circumstances' when really the blocks are of your own making?

Chapter 16

It's only when you can face death that you're ready to live

Fear is at the heart of all our emotional problems. And there is one thing that we fear more than anything else – our own death! Much of our time – usually subconsciously – is spent worrying about the inevitable. We know that we're going to die sooner or later. And that latent, primitive fear – buried deep within the subconscious – drives us, causing us to live in fear rather than joy. But by shifting perspective, we can begin to see that through death, life has meaning.

The reason we fear dying is that we're afraid of no longer existing – afraid that 'I' will no longer matter. And the more we try to consciously avoid a thought, the more it underpins our thinking. This is because the subconscious mind cannot process a negative command – try not thinking of a purple tiger! All the time we're trying to avoid a thought; we're actually being driven by it, even though we may not be aware of it. As we get older, we get better at burying our fears, believing – like the proverbial ostrich – that if we can't see them, then they're not really there. Whole industries are created to help us bury our fears – and make others rich at our expense! Alcohol, TV and computer games – indeed anything that prevents us from living in the moment – may dull our fearful minds but they also inhibit our creative stirrings and reduce our ability to reach our full potential!

Guru Success Tip

The death of a situation often means the birth of a new one!

Try this experiment. Ask a friend if they're happy in their own company – and then turn up the heat a bit by suggesting they spend a day on their own, with no reading material, music or TV for company. You'll be shocked by just how many people recoil in horror! Being with nothing and nobody but yourself is very strange. Once I did a three day 'solace' – which meant plenty of meditation and complete silence – and was surprised to find just how much negativity it brought up. It wasn't just keeping quiet that I found difficult (!) but with no communication with anybody whatsoever, I began to feel not only abandoned but as though I'd ceased to exist. I felt disconnected from everyone around me. In fact the whole solace experience felt as though I was going through a personal mini-death – but with no one to mourn my passing!

Death is the last taboo in society. And yet in reality it's our greatest teacher. Once we can face up to death and understand it for what it is – and what it isn't – then we can transcend our fears and get on with living life. Death teaches us what's important. We could even acknowledge death as the greatest *motivator* of all – reminding us that we live within time constraints. We use the term 'deadline' to motivate ourselves to finish a particular project and in the same way we can use our own demise as an even bigger call to action.

Sometimes, if we look hard enough, the death of a loved one brings with it unforeseen gifts. After all, it was only when my grandparents – who I was very close to – died within six months of each other that I was prompted to try counselling. And of course, there are other types of 'mini-death' that also affect us, like the end of a relationship or being made redundant, for example.

It had felt like the end of life as I'd known it when I found myself being unceremoniously sacked by the managing director of the advertising agency where I'd worked for the best part of two years. His reason for getting rid of me was that I hadn't met my targets – but we both knew that he'd never given me any! To be fair, I'd not been a great fan of how the company had treated its staff – or indeed its clients. On more than one occasion, the MD and I had nearly come to blows because I felt he was overcharging clients. Looking back, I didn't have the courage to give up a well-paying job to go self-employed – but his sacking me left me with little choice. As I was to think to myself later, it was the best decision he'd ever made!

In my work with company directors and senior management teams, I've taught that death is not only our teacher, but also our greatest motivator. With no death, there can be no life. Life and death are the two sides of the same coin. When you're prepared to face the unthinkable, somehow it becomes easier to discern what makes you feel fulfilled in life (that's when you feel really alive) and what makes you feel trapped (those are the things that make you feel dead on your feet!).

LIFE IN THE COMFORT ZONE IS A LIVING DEATH …

You're unique, so it stands to reason that your life will be unique too. Are you living your life according to your soul's call – or are you wasting precious time trying to live according to what your family or society dictates?

Facing up to your death is the gateway to freedom. Knowing that the world will continue whether or not you're in it helps you break free from the need to conform to earn approval. Recognising the gift in your own death, you can afford to break 'the rules' as gaining approval from others and feeling secure are no longer your priorities. People who've lived through wars report that in spite of the terror, there was a real appreciation of life, together with an almost primitive drive to live each moment as though it really might be the last!

Embracing true freedom can be frightening – not least because we know that in order to live up to our full potential, our lives will irrevocably change. While most of us may not be control freaks, we do tend to value a sense of control over our lives – and for most of us 'control' equals 'comfort zone'! Have you ever wondered about your comfort zones? Where do you conform to other people's expectations? What would you do in life if you knew that failure simply wasn't a possibility?

Early on in my career, I worked on the in-house newspaper for a high street bank. On my first day in my new job, I was stunned by the strict staff grading systems – for example, if you were a particular grade you were entitled to a brown chair rather than a grey one. I thought it was the in-house joke, but I was soon to discover that status and hierarchy were absolutely no laughing matter! Equally jaw-dropping was the reverence people held for their colleagues who'd held exactly the same job for years.

'Bill', I was told in hushed tones, 'deserves a lot of respect. He's got more than 30 years' experience.' After quietly studying Bill for a couple of weeks, I thought it more likely Bill actually had one year's experience, which he'd repeated 30 times!

Maybe Bill had remained in the same job because he simply loved what he was doing. However, in a later conversation when I asked him what he liked about his job, he confessed that it wasn't his career that kept him with the bank – but his pension! Clearly, he wasn't to know what would happen to pensions in the following years – but how many of us are like Bill, prostituting our souls for the sake of money and potential security?

Fear makes us hang on to what we've got. It's as though we're not sure enough of ourselves to believe that there really could be something better out there for us! Fear of failure is a common phenomenon but fear of success is equally debilitating. To understand the latter, you have to realise that with success comes upheaval and change. How would your family and friends react to you being super-successful?

Would they all be delighted for you – or would some be jealous of the rewards you were enjoying? Perhaps some of them would be afraid that you'd 'leave them behind' – and in a bid to avoid this pain, they'd reject you first! Nobody likes rejection, so in a bid to avoid it, we instead avoid creating the success that could create the rejection we fear. Never mind that we shoot ourselves at the same time!

> **Guru Success Tip**
>
> Make sure that you get the most out of life by grabbing at all the experiences life has to offer – and, above all, avoid existing merely in the comfort zone!

Try turning the tables for a moment. And be honest! How would you feel if a friend you're close to suddenly became super-successful – or was just lucky enough to win the lottery? Would you be genuinely pleased for them or would you feel the stirrings of the green-eyed monster? Fast forward the video a little – if they were to move to a bigger house, eat out at more expensive places and start to enjoy exotic holidays, how long would you actually remain in close contact?

Only a strong person, someone who is sure about their own personal purpose in life, can be genuinely happy about someone else's success. Rather than feeling threatened, he or she will be inspired to even greater personal achievement. In this kind of relationship, each brings out the best in the other. How many inspiring relationships like this do you have? And who can you think of who drags you down through their negativity? Can you really afford to have them in your life? Of course, I'm not suggesting that you should dump everyone who doesn't have a relentlessly positive attitude – but just being aware of why people behave the way they do can be helpful when you're trying to understand their bewildering behaviour and put-downs!

EVERY MOMENT OF OUR LIVES IS A SPIRITUAL CHOICE POINT …

The decisions we take today dictate the life that we live tomorrow. Good decisions, bad decisions – all have their consequences. The best decisions aren't always the ones that everyone tells you are logical – sometimes they're the crazy ones that somehow just make your heart sing! Often those decisions are thrust upon us, as though the only way we can be encouraged to 'wake up' is through our pain. Do you find when life is comfortable that you're coasting? We only get stretched through strife! We only find out just how much we're capable of achieving by coming through the difficult times.

Of course, sometimes the pain can be almost unbearable – and yet as the old adage goes, we only get given what we're capable of dealing with! I've had sessions with clients who've had suicides amongst friends and family – and their pain has been overwhelming. And yet, by introducing the spiritual dimension into the equation, healing does, almost miraculously, start to take place.

It helps to think of yourself as a spiritual being having a human experience, rather than as a human being having a spiritual experience. From this perspective you can see that some of the pain we experience in the human realms is only temporary – and an aid to our remembering who we really are at our core. We carry our spiritual essence within us, although all too often it's carefully hidden from view. As we become more spiritually aware, we become able to shine our 'light' more brightly. And when we begin to shine more brightly, we begin to attract the right people and opportunities to us, making our lives run more smoothly, more serenely, more happily!

Finally, I'd like to leave you with this thought, 'If you're too busy being busy, then you've no time to be busy being!' And guess which state brings happiness and freedom?

Chapter 17

Are you simply a figment of your imagination?

*M*ore than one of the male delegates, clearly moved by their soul journey experience, had quietly dug into their trouser pockets hoping to find a handkerchief. It was Matt who, without any prompting from me, decided to share with the others what he'd learned.

'I can't believe where going to my funeral has taken me', he said, his voice cracking slightly with emotion. 'None of you know this but for a while things haven't been very good at home. Actually, they'd got so bad that I was pretty tempted recently to start an affair. If I'm honest it was only my fear of being found out that stopped me. It seemed to me that my wife and I were growing apart, at least that what she's always telling me! I think she resents the amount of effort I put into work and I guess I do spend quite a lot of time away from home. Somehow everything seemed to change between us after we had our son, Ben. For me, it was almost as though I'd lost my wife – and in her place I'd been forced to live with someone completely different! Before, she'd always been great fun and had shared my sense of adventure – but now she's so focused on Ben that it's almost as if she doesn't have any time for me. Or at least, that's how I used to feel – up until about an hour ago!'

'But when you took me to my funeral, I saw that my wife wasn't there. It was as though she'd ceased to be a part of my life. From that point in the future, looking back, I realised that I'd gone on to have a string of affairs. She put up with a lot but then she met someone new, someone who treated her with respect. I lost her for ever. It was when I saw her with her new husband that I realised just how much I'd truly lost. My heart was broken and I never really got over it. And, of course, I lost my son too. The two people I really loved weren't there, at my funeral, and it was all down to me!'

Jenny, who'd been sitting next to Matt, quietly put her hand on his arm. At this gesture of simple kindness, a couple of tears escaped from Matt's already shiny eyes. I knew this was 'big' for Matt, and that the others would be learning just as much from the experience. We all remained quiet, waiting patiently for him to gain his composure so that he could go on with his story.

'But your voice Olivia, started to filter through the misery I was feeling. When you said "Imagine that you've been given a second chance to live the rest of your life," I knew that things really could be different. Having tasted life without my wife and son, I knew that I didn't want that scenario to become a reality. I guess I've got a lot of making-up to do with my wife …'

For Matt, this had been a life changing moment. It had been a privilege to share it with him.

'Great work Matt', I said and turning to the rest of the room added, 'and remember, we get to choose how our life pans out in each and every moment. We live in the present only – but the choices you make in your present absolutely affect your future.'

Buying a little time to give Matt a chance to recover, I picked up a bottle of sparkling water from the table and began to refill everyone's glasses.

'So, here's a thought for you', I said when once again I was standing at the front of the room. 'Are you simply a figment of your imagination?'

Bewildered looks crossed the faces of most of the delegates, so I decided to help them out a little. It was getting quite late in the afternoon but as there was a lot for us to get through the following day, I couldn't afford to call a halt to the proceedings just yet.

'This is the last topic for today, I promise!' I said reassuringly. 'And what we're going to be discussing is the role of our ego! Does anybody have any news, views, gossip or scandal about the ego?'

Pete was the first to venture a response. 'I suppose the ego is the part of us that gets us into trouble?' he hazarded.

Everyone laughed. 'Sure, in a way, you're right. But I'm not into ego bashing. We need our egos – and more than you think. And they're responsible for a lot more than making sure that we keep clean and smell good!

'Everything – as we've already discussed at length – that we experience is processed according to our beliefs and values. No two people experience the world in the same way. You could even go as far as to say that we're the product of our very own histories. Or maybe it would be more accurate to say that our **ego** is the product of our history, while our soul, or inner guru, is the seed of our potential!'

I'd paused for a few minutes, waiting for my message to sink in.

'Our egos serve as camouflage – hiding the guru spark that waits to be ignited by our search for personal purpose or meaning. Many of us waste a great deal of time searching for the answers outside of ourselves, when all the time we're oblivious to the fact that we're carrying them around within us, hidden from view. It's all too easy to travel the world, or explore a variety of religions, hoping to "find yourself" – but wherever you go, you're still there! At the end of the day, you'll never be able to find what you're seeking outside *of yourself, although of course you may be lucky enough to pick up some useful pointers along the way.'*

As I was speaking, a wonderful story came to mind concerning the Sufi sage, Mulla Nasrudin, whose exploits illuminate the human condition with humour and a rich mysticism. I decided to share it with the delegates to illustrate my point. 'One night Nasrudin is out in the street looking for his key. A friend passes by and asks if he can help. "Exactly where did you drop your key?" asks the friend. "In my house," replies Nasrudin. "So why are you looking for it here, then?" asks his puzzled friend. "Well," replies Nasrudin, "it's pitch dark in my house, but out here I can see what I'm doing!"'

A smile of amusement lit the faces around the room. I swiftly followed it up with a question. 'How many people do you know who are looking for the answers outside of themselves? A great clue is to see whether people take responsibility for themselves and their actions, or whether they prefer to blame others. In fact, we might benefit from applying the question to ourselves too!'

I went on to explain that by shifting responsibility for themselves on to others, blamers tend to see themselves merely as victims of circumstance. But when you're blaming others, you're not taking responsibility for your own life experience which means that effectively, you're simply giving your power away. I added that, interestingly, what goes on outside of us is often a reflection of what's going on inside too.

As I said this, the memory of a most peculiar incident floated into my mind, as if from nowhere. Normally, I trust my intuition implicitly but I had serious reservations about sharing this particular story. Nonetheless, I'd made a pact to follow my heart on that night way back in Thailand and I wasn't about to get cold feet now …

'Let me give you a really "far out" example of what I'm talking about. A great friend of mine and I were due to do a joint "before dinner presentation" for a key client's national sales team. We'd left plenty of time to get to

the hotel but our journey from the outset had been a catalogue of disaster. We'd been caught in traffic three times already – twice in heavy road works and once because of a nasty accident. And by this point we were only half way there! I tried to ring the client to explain our predicament but I couldn't get any answer. I knew that we'd no hope of arriving for our time slot of half past seven and just prayed that perhaps we'd be able to do our "gig" after dinner instead. I've always hated being late and somehow it was even worse when a well-liked and respected client was involved. By my estimate, if we were lucky, we'd get there by half past nine. And that was if we were lucky …

'But I made that estimate before the traffic started to slow yet again. What made it worse was that this time my car – yes, my beloved old convertible – started overheating. For me, there was a simple solution: put the heating full on and take the roof down. I'd done it many times before. But I hadn't reckoned on my friend's obsession with her hair. I thought she was only joking when she said she'd rather stick needles in her eyes than go in my car with the roof down and let her beautiful locks be blown to the winds. But I was soon to realise that she hadn't been joking at all. Worse, her mounting fury triggered my sense of the absurd, with the result that I started laughing! Well, that was the last straw. My friend started to let rip and, at the same time, the traffic in front came to a complete standstill. We didn't move an inch for about 20 minutes – and all the while, my friend was doing her best to turn the air blue!

'Suddenly, a really strange thought began to dawn on me. My friend had done a lot of mystical study in her life and we both knew the power that our thoughts can have on our environment. Could it be that she was actually blocking the traffic with her fury? It sounded absurd but I checked my theory with her, and her eyes lit up. She agreed that maybe I had a point! I've always admired her open-mindedness and she didn't let me down. "Why don't you take me through a guided visualisation; maybe we can free the traffic that way?" she asked.

'It was all too absurd for words – but by that point we had nothing left to lose. So, picture the scene, there we were, me behind the wheel talking her

down into a state of light relaxation! It didn't take long – she'd had years of practice getting into an altered state. Not quite sure where to take it next, I grasped at straws and asked her to picture us flying above the traffic queue. I'd only been suggesting this to her for a couple of minutes when, to my utter amazement, the traffic began slowly to move. Was it coincidence? Who cared? I carried on talking to her about flying freely and saw that a little way ahead, there was one clear lane. In seconds we were moving. All the traffic around us still seemed to be stuck and yet somehow we were moving. I'll never forget that drive – and nor will she!'

Jenny in particular seemed amazed by the story. 'So what happened? What time did you arrive?'

'To this day, I don't know how it all happened. One minute we had another two hours to go – providing there were no further hold-ups – yet it seemed as though in the next minute we'd actually arrived! In fact, when I checked my watch, we'd done the journey in just 40 minutes – and had even arrived in good time to do our presentation on schedule!'

Leaning over to help himself to a biscuit, Pete said, 'I suppose it's just another demonstration of what you were saying earlier. It would seem that what we think about really can have an effect on what we experience in life!'

'Sure', I replied, and you'll be hearing some more strange-but-true stories tomorrow, so watch this space!'

Points to ponder as you start to ...
Be your own guru

1 Every time you need to make a decision today, stop and think whether the decision is coming from your ego or your inner guru. (A great clue is how the decision makes you feel – comfortable but bored or slightly uncomfortable but alive!)

2 When you start to judge someone else – whether it's for what they're wearing or what they're doing, realise that it's your ego that's doing the judging! Rather than seeing yourself as separate to the other person, try – just for the fun of it – to see what you and they have in common.

3 How much are you driven by your ego's need for recognition and approval? How would your life be if you could drop these needs and simply get on with the business of living? Would you be happier? Would you feel freer, more fulfilled?

Chapter 18

Are you the product of your history or your potential?

Survival of the species is one of the strongest, most powerful and yet most primitive drivers. Perhaps knowing that we leave a legacy through our children helps us feel immortal. Yet in many ways this driver, combined with our focus on just getting through each day in order to pay the bills at the end of the month, prevents us from lifting the veil to discover who we really are – and even more importantly, who we're capable of being.

As we've already seen, one of our biggest fears in life is rejection – and by conforming we hope to reduce that risk. But as we start to mature – and begin asking ourselves the more deep and meaningful questions in life, the conformity that kept us safe starts instead to stifle and strangle us. But we can't make any headway until we begin to understand that *our separateness is the illusion …*

In the end, how you live your life comes down to choice. Apart from the only certainties in life – death and taxes – you absolutely *do* have free will. Of course, there are things over which we have no seeming control, and – in insurance speak – these are referred to as 'acts of God'. However, we have a lot more influence on our lives than we perhaps care to admit! If our ego is the sum total of our history and our soul spark is the seed of our potential, then when everything's distilled down to its essence, the choice is this: Do you live the life dictated by your past – or by your potential? Deciding whether to live from ego or

> **Guru Success Tip**
>
> Know that what seems scary today will look like child's play tomorrow – dare yourself to stretch your comfort zone!

potential is the choice point that we find ourselves at every moment in every day, no matter our age, gender, or financial circumstances.

But despite what you may be thinking, your ego has a very valid role to play in your life. And it's not just about keeping you grounded and reminding you to take a regular shower! As well as giving us a sense of identity, the ego also gives us our drive, our ambition and our desire for life.

But, the real reason for the ego's existence is much more important. The ego's role is actually far more *selfless* than we've ever been led to believe – and it deserves all the credit for enabling us to grow, change and even ultimately reach enlightenment. How? The ego teaches us who we are – by helping us understand who we are not.

We live in a world of duality – and enlightenment occurs the moment we recognise the oneness of all that is. It's as simple and as complicated as that. In order to discover who we are, we need to discover who we are not. Your ego serves you in this endeavour.

Our world of duality helps us to understand the world around us by enabling us to distinguish what something is through its opposite – what a thing is not. To know that something is hot, for example, you need to have experienced cold. Otherwise it simply 'is'. And what simply 'is' we take for granted, never questioning it, never growing beyond it. I saw a cartoon once that illustrates the point perfectly. Two goldfish were swimming in a goldfish bowl. One of them was asking the other, 'What's water?'

In the same way that you're not your physical body, you're not your ego. Someone once said that if you were put in a room that was completely white, and you were dressed from head to toe in white, it wouldn't be long before you went insane. The reason, apparently, is because you'd have no reference point for where you 'begin' and where you 'end'. Paint a black dot on the wall, however, and immediately you'd be able to recognise it as being something different to everything else. We're back to our world of duality again. In the same way, your ego not only provides you with a reference point of who you're not – but through studying and observing it, you can create a route map for successful personal growth.

For this reason, we most definitely need our ego, in the same way that a space rocket needs the booster rocket for lift-off. But once we achieve full flight, the booster rocket (or in our case, our ego) must be jettisoned or it'll weigh us down, causing us to crash.

The ego begins to form from the moment we're born and by creating a personal identity, it helps us to understand our boundaries. In this way, the ego teaches us that we're 'separate'. Indeed, on this three-dimensional earth plane, we *are* separate – which is probably why, in society, the ego rules! Our spiritual quest in life – whether we're aware of it or not – is to transcend the separateness and rediscover the oneness. Or, in other words, the spiritual path is about seeking to create unity where duality currently exists.

It's our ability to make sense of what we perceive through our senses that brings the ego to life and causes us to *feel* separate. In this way we're different from animals, which have no ego. Pets are renowned for their ability to give unconditional love – and even ferocious lions are only 'being' what their genes programme them to be! By believing that we're separate and that we're not a part of the whole, we're only too aware that at any moment, our very existence could swiftly come to an end.

The first step to transcending our separateness and embracing the whole – and taking our rightful place within it – is to love and accept ourselves totally. The road to self-acceptance and the path of enlightenment are one and the same. Accepting the ego as our heavily disguised teacher enables us to embark – with a lighter heart – on the road to self-discovery. And we can take refuge in the fact that every single experience – whether positive or negative – will aid our learning. The trick is to begin letting go of self-hatred and instead replace it with self-love. By doing this, we can even elevate the ego to its proper place of part-time spiritual teacher!

IT'S TIME TO FINALLY GROW UP ...

Do you remember being a child? Of course you do, and the essence of you is still the same, even though your physical body has matured and grown bigger.

However, here comes the rub. As a child, you were used to looking up to other people (you had to, you were smaller) and you began to recognise that these authority figures had power over you. While your parents or guardians gave you security by providing food and shelter, your teachers also had the power to make you feel clever or stupid – and to keep you in after school! Because you grew used to being in the lower subordinate position, you began to take it for granted that other people knew more than you and that they had the right to wield their power over you.

Scarily, because it's still the same 'you' looking 'outwards', unless you've consciously worked on changing your earlier patterning, the chances are that this feeling of being less powerful has never gone away. No wonder so many of us lack self-confidence. And, of course, the paradox here is that although you've probably never realised it, to everyone around you – who still feel like children themselves – you're the 'adult', the powerful, all-knowing one.

If you don't believe me, then take a trip down memory lane and visit your old school. You'll be amazed at how small – and unthreatening – everything seems, from the desks and chairs to the teachers themselves! What's amazing is that the memories of everything to do with childhood loom much larger than the reality – and yet, unless we consciously review our subconscious patterns, they can have serious consequences for us in adulthood, as my client David had come to experience.

David had wanted all his life to be recognised as a 'somebody' – and it was this subconscious drive which led to him launching his own business ten years ago. And while David's bull-headed determination helped him make a modest success of his company, he was beginning to realise that, whilst he was working hard, he wasn't achieving the results that he'd originally anticipated.

Understanding that he needed to find a way to work 'smarter' rather than harder, David decided to see if the services of a business coach could help him discover the root of the problem. After listening to his story, I asked him how he promoted his company to potential clients. Sadly, his answer came as no surprise. With a wry smile, he admitted that he had no marketing goals and rather than work to a plan, he'd adopted a scatter-gun approach with regard to his promotional activities.

Clearly, he'd been wasting both his time and the company's money. After a little more discussion, we started getting closer to the nub of the problem. David had been spending his marketing budget in the places where his family and colleagues – all of whom he wanted to impress – would see his name in lights. However, the problem was that his target audience didn't read the same publications as his family and colleagues! To his chagrin, David was also embarrassed to admit that he'd agreed to sponsor a local football team for the next two years – in return for their wearing his corporate colours and logo. He had no choice but to laugh when I asked him whether any potential customers were likely to play for – or support – the local team. 'I guess that's unlikely', he replied, 'my company makes walking frames for the elderly and infirm!'

I asked David who he was really trying to impress with his sponsorship deal. After looking blankly at me, the truth slowly began to dawn – he was trying to impress himself. With David's agreement, I guided him into a light state of hypnosis – with the aim of discovering the root cause of his lack of confidence. It wasn't long before we found the answer. The youngest of three clever – and sporty – brothers, he felt inferior and wanted to prove himself. On one hand he was naturally shy and retiring but on the other, he was also driven by an overwhelming need for recognition, at whatever cost to himself. It was a pattern that had repeated itself throughout his life. In truth, David had set up his business in a bid to achieve recognition – and he'd bought a number of flashy suits and a brand new car for the same reason!

Working at the subconscious level with David, we managed to reframe his beliefs about himself – and his place in the world. After our session, David agreed that, as well as learning from the past, he also intended his future to be completely different. He recognised that, now he accepted himself, he could choose to take on a true leadership role – one where he put his customers' needs first rather than those of his ego!

Sadly, the essence of David's story isn't unusual. Many people – it could even be you, your partner or your boss – are running on past-their-sell-by-date subconscious software. Just how many fallings-out are due to people acting out of their childhood memories rather than in-the-now reality?

Section 3

You! You! You!

Until I understand you, and you understand me – how can you and I create 'WE'?

Chapter 19
Different views, same world

*A*s I looked around the room, I was delighted to see that the delegates looked eager and refreshed from a good night's sleep. Over the mid-morning coffee break, they would go on to tell me that they'd all been so exhausted from the previous day that after dinner and a nightcap, they'd all been tucked up in bed by ten!

I also observed that there was a real sense of bonding between them all. Before, they had seemed more like a collection of individuals – but the experience of sharing such an intense journey together was having a profound impact on the psyche of the group as a whole.

As these thoughts were running through my mind, I went up to the flip chart and with a large black marker pen, I wrote:

60% = visual

10% = audio

30% = kinesthetic

'In the western world, about 60% of people think visually, or in other words they tend to think in pictures. Before I go on, remember that none of these "processing" modalities are any better than any other. They're just different – and you may also care to know at this point that most of us have a primary and secondary style.

'Anyway, back to the visual representational system. Visual people are great at grasping an outline concept quickly but their minds tend to wander when presented with too many fine details, especially when issued with verbal instructions. You can usually tell the type of people who are visual – they're the ones who always dress for show! They're also prone to using their hands a lot to show you what they mean when they're talking. They're often quite neat and organised and to speak in their language you need to "paint a picture" for them or at least help them "see the point." What other kind of words do you think visual people would be inclined to use?' I asked the group.

Everyone started calling out words at once. 'I need to get a perspective on …'; 'I take a dim view of that …'; 'In my mind's eye …'; 'That's a short-sighted perspective …'

'Great – you get the picture', I said, laughingly adding, 'and from that remark you'd be right, I'm primarily visual! Next, let's look at the audio people. As you can see, few people are primarily audio in their thinking – which means that they often feel misunderstood. Several audio people have told me that it's as though they're speaking a different language to everyone else and now you can see why!

'Audio people are good at listening to verbal instructions and are able to repeat things back to you easily. Not surprisingly, they often like music and can talk for hours on the phone! They tend to memorise by breaking things down into chunks, procedures and sequences. Audio people tend to respond to particular tones of voice and like to hear what you have to say about something. It pays to make things "sound right" to audio people. What other words do you think they might be inclined to use?'

Again, more suggestions came from the floor. 'The engine purrs like a kitten ...'; 'It's loud and clear ...'; "He voiced an opinion ..." 'We're tuned in to the same wavelength ...';

'Fantastic, this is all obviously ringing a bell for you guys!' Pausing to take a sip from my glass of water, I continued, 'And finally we come to the kinesthetic style of thinking. Before you ask, kinesthetic is just a posh word for "feeling" – not so much emotionally but in the sense of being aware of physical sensations. You can usually tell kinesthetic people from the way they're dressed too – but only because they dress from the feet upwards. First they'll choose a pair of comfortable shoes and then they'll work their way upwards from there! They often tend to move and speak very s-l-o-w-l-y, which can really wind up their visual colleagues who are more likely to talk very quickly. They understand a concept either by trying it out for themselves or at least "walking through it" in their mind's eye. They'll be more interested in what you have to say if it "feels" right!'

I then went on to remind the delegates again that there was no better or worse thinking style, and that they were simply different. 'However', I continued, 'there is the potential for the different styles to fall out with other.'

Having already determined that Matt was pretty visual – his carefully gelled hair, checked shirt and shiny shoes had told me that from the moment I'd met him, I went up to him and stood close to his chair. 'Visual people', I explained, 'like to have a lot of personal space around them and I dare say that Matt feels I'm invading his space right now!'

'Well, I didn't want to be rude – but now you've said it, yes, you are!'

'But watch this ...' And as the words were coming out of my mouth, I walked over to Pete, who I'd worked out from his language patterns was primarily kinesthetic. As I moved closer and closer to him, he didn't move a muscle – not even when I dramatically threw my arms around him. 'And that doesn't bother you at all Pete, does it?'

'Most certainly not', he gallantly replied.

'There is one more thinking system and this is referred to as auditory digital. All of us tend to operate with this style from time to time, as really it's the language of "process". For example, when you're giving someone directions, you're bringing your auditory digital processing system into play. But, for now, we're going to concentrate on the other three representational systems.'

Jenny had her head in her hands, and she was wearing a bemused look on her face. 'To be honest', she said, 'I feel as though I fit into all the categories – maybe I just don't know who I am', she added, laughing.

'Some people are naturally lucky and do seem to be quite at home with all the different thinking types. While this can make it easier to communicate and get on well with everyone, do you sometimes find that you end up playing the mediator role rather than standing up for what you believe in?'

'Too right!' she laughed again. 'Worse, it's not just the different perspectives that I can understand but I also find myself in empathy with just about everyone I come across. To be honest, while this aspect of my personality helps me form relationships with clients, it does make it much harder for me to stand up for myself in personal situations. I can see other people's point of view so clearly that I tend to overlook mine!'

It was a great learning experience. After our initial coaching session together, Jenny knew that she had the right to make sure that her needs were part of the equation too. I suggested that she consider consciously focusing on creating win–win situations – whereas to date many of her dialogues had ended in lose–win, with her on the losing end!

'OK', I continued, 'so we've already established that people approach things pretty differently. But, there's a lot more to it than that. I want you to recall how yesterday we talked about our value and belief systems. As you know, we all judge events, situations and people against our experiences. Let me prove it to you. Think of someone whom you really didn't like at school. What was their name? Now, think back to a time when you met someone with the same name for the first time. I'll bet that, without quite knowing why, you found it a little harder to warm to that person than you *normally would. Or you made them jump through more hoops to prove their worthiness to you …'*

Pete smiled. 'Yes, thinking about it, it's true! We had a horrible boy at school called Simon, who really made my life a misery. Now, when I meet someone called Simon, the barriers tend to go up automatically! But when you stop to think about it, it does seem a bit unfair on the poor new person.'

*'Yes', I agreed with him. 'It **is** unfair – but at least now, unlike most people, you're aware of it!'*

'And maybe' Jenny pointed out, 'that's why some people just don't seem to like us very much at all either, simply because we remind them of somebody else from their past. Presumably, it's not just names that trigger us – but also the tone of someone's voice or the way they look?'

'Got it in one again, Jenny', I replied.

Moving back to my place at the front of the room, I continued, 'Let's look at some of the other potential difficulties. Remember I said that visual people tend to speak fast, while kinesthetic people speak more slowly? Sometimes visuals mistake the slowness for stupidity – and step in to finish their sentences for them. As you can imagine, far from being grateful, the kinesthetics resent this, feeling that they're being disrespected.

'Also, visuals tend to look at things from the "bigger picture" perspective. Often they'll go from problem to solution in one hit – without taking the time to explain their working out to their audio and kinesthetic colleagues. And the latter, far from being impressed, tend to think that the visual people are all mouth and no trousers! Visuals also tend to speak quicker as they get more excited, often not even finishing sentences off properly. Other visuals won't be bothered by this because they're used to thinking and speaking in a similar kind of verbal shorthand, although of course misunderstandings can arise when two visuals are seeing completely different pictures. It's easy to see how arguments start – and it's not even because of what we say but because of the way we're saying it!'

This time it was Pete's turn to start laughing. 'I've just realised, I'm more of a kinesthetic and my boss is highly visual. He always seems to be impatient and he does finish my sentences off for me – and you're right, I do find it very annoying! I guess we're lucky we haven't come to blows yet …'

'That's a great point Pete – I'm sure you'd all agree that there's plenty of scope for falling out in our everyday lives – let alone when we have to go into those situations we find stressful!

'The trick really is to understand that if you're seeking to influence someone then you need to adapt your way of communicating into their preferred style. That's the way to create rapport. I'm not suggesting that you shouldn't be anyone other than who you are but after all, when you go on holiday to France, the French seem to appreciate it when you try to speak their language – and they certainly prefer it to you shouting louder in English!'

'Isn't influencing someone manipulative?' asked Jenny.

'Good point. Does anyone know the difference between influence and manipulation?'

*No one answered, so I continued, 'If I seek to **influence** you, I want what's in both yours and my best interests. However if I want to **manipulate** you, then I want you to do what's in my best interests but not in yours. Get the difference?*

'And if you really want to succeed in life, the thing to remember is that the other person always needs to know – even if its only subconsciously – what's in it for them. If you find out what someone else wants to achieve – and you help them get there then, my friends, the world most definitely is your oyster!'

It seemed like a good time to break for lunch. 'We'll be looking more into relationships this afternoon – and you're going to be stunned when you discover how to tap into your intuition and the impact that can have on your relationships …'

Points to ponder as you start to ...
Be your own guru

1 Listen to the types of language patterns people use. Do they use visual, audio or feeling types of language?

2 When you meet someone new, become a personal detective and see how many clues you can pick up about their personality. You'll find out more by listening to how they speak, their body language and what they're wearing. Further clues can be picked up by looking closely at someone's environment. Is there evidence of sporting prowess (trophies) a love of travel (souvenirs) or are they more 'homebodies' with lots of family and friends' pictures displayed everywhere?

3 Start becoming more aware of points of commonality. Think about your friends and list ten things you have in common with them. Now think about people you've found it harder to connect with and do your best to find ten things in common with them too. You'll probably feel better disposed towards them if you can succeed in this – and as you know, people tend to feel the same way about you as you do about them, so looking for reasons to get on with someone absolutely has to be in your best interests!

Chapter 20
It's our differences which make life so exciting

I t's only when we really get to understand ourselves that we're in a position to begin understanding other people. While we may want similar things in life – health, happiness, loving relationships, financial freedom – we all go about getting them in different ways, according to our personality types.

While there are many great psychometric tools out there, I personally get a little uncomfortable with putting people into boxes. After all, it's our inner spark that's pure potential. When we're operating from our inner spark, we're operating from something much bigger than ourselves. Swiss psychiatrist Carl Jung referred to this as the 'collective unconscious'. His thinking was that we're all able to tap into a shared pool of memories, ideas and ways of thinking that come from the life experience not only of our ancestors but also from the entire human race!

Of course, when it comes to understanding our personalities, we're likely to get into the great 'nature versus nurture' debate. Are we born the way we are, or does life make us that way? Great quantities of research exist which prove beyond any doubt both sides of the argument, which at the end of the day leaves us none the wiser! Common sense would suggest that it's a blend of both nature and nurture that makes us who we are – and understanding one's own potential strengths and foibles, together with those of other people, gives us a leg up on the ladder to happiness and success.

Guru Success Tip

Know that it's our differences which make the difference – in relationships, at work and in life. Celebrate your differences – they're what make you unique!

As well as our preferences for understanding – and choosing to operate within – the world in a certain way, there's also a myriad of additional elements that contribute to making us who we are. The most fundamental are how we make sense of the world, how we process our thinking and how we communicate.

One of the most exciting systems for understanding our differences – and our points of commonality – is Neuro-Linguistic Programming (NLP), which has been dubbed the 'science of success'. In much the same way that we programme computers, NLP ('Neuro' roughly translates from the Greek as 'mind', while the root of 'Linguistic' comes from the Latin for 'language') is based on the premise that we can programme ourselves for excellence – through our use of language, and sensory inputs like sights, sounds and feelings.

CREATING EFFECTIVE RELATIONSHIPS …

The quality of our relationships determines whether we succeed or fail in life. Until we have an understanding of – and a great relationship with – ourselves, our relationships with others will always be slightly tainted. It's only when we learn to accept and then love ourselves that we'll stop being driven by our ego. Now, while we know that the ego serves a great purpose – by teaching us who're not – it's less helpful when it comes to relationships. In relationships, the ego is either driven by its self-importance or its lack of self-worth. Both of these are illusory and by definition, illusion is 'not truth' – relationships that are built on a structure of 'not truth' always come unstuck (to a greater or lesser degree) at some point.

It's also worth noting that we can only give to others what we have ourselves. If I have no money, then how can I give you any? In the same way, if I have no trust for myself, then how can I trust you? If I have no love for myself, then how can I love you? If I don't want what's best for me, then how can I want what's best for you? Of course, we might go to considerable lengths to cover up our deficiencies but we're doing that again to create an illusion, recognising that if we were to be our 'true' miserable selves, then no-one would want to spend any time with us at all! However, when we learn to accept and love ourselves, we bring those same attitudes into our dealings with other people – meaning that, at last, we can afford to live 'in truth'. When we're living in truth, we have integrity – and however much we try to hide it, people pick up intuitively whether or not we're coming from 'the right place'. If we're not, without quite knowing why, other people will sense that we're incongruent – or in other words, our words don't match our behaviours. Incongruency, not surprisingly, tends to beget lack of trust, which in turn begets poor relationships!

Guru Success Tip

No matter how hard you try, you can never change anyone else. The only person you can change is yourself. However, when you change, you'll notice that the dynamics of the relationship change too!

Trust is the keystone of great relationships – and if the relationship is to survive in the long term, that trust must be based on authenticity and integrity – rather than on the more superficial qualities of charisma and instant rapport building skills for which NLP is renowned. There's nothing wrong with the latter, as long as the desire is to influence rather than to manipulate. Who dictates whether you influence or manipulate? You do! (And if nothing else, it's always useful to know how other people could be using their skills of persuasion on you!)

One of the key tenets of NLP is that *'people like people who like them, and who are like them'*. In other words, we tend to immediately connect with people with whom we feel an inexplicable bond. While opposites may attract, the old adage teaches us that 'birds of a feather, fly together'. Establishing rapport then, is little more than finding the points of commonality. Think back to your first meeting with someone with whom you went on to forge a strong relationship. As you both discovered that you had more and more in common, didn't you feel a growing bond? Now think about someone with whom you have a less good relationship, or who for some reason you don't quite trust. Without even realising it, you'll start to look for all the points of difference – which will somehow justify (to yourself) your lack of liking for the other person.

Prejudice, racial hatred and religious intolerance arise only as a result of the fact that we're educated (through our backgrounds, our experiences and the media) to focus on the elements that separate us. In the same way that you'd go mad in the all-white room I mentioned earlier, we look for the points of difference in people outside of our group so that we can forge stronger bonds with our own tribe, with whom we feel safe. It's the stuff of which gangs are made. The attitude of 'us against the rest of the world' is the glue that binds gangs – and even some marriages – and we indulge in this kind of thinking because it soothes our ego, which above all else wants to feel that it belongs.

To achieve rapport with someone, simply look for the points of commonality. You don't have to have known someone for years – in fact you can establish rapport with a complete stranger within a couple of minutes! This is done by matching and mirroring the language – verbal and physical – patterns of the person with whom you want to establish the relationship. (And yes, you can establish rapport with a whole group of people. Simply establish who the leader of the group is and create rapport with them. Once you've got rapport with him or her, everyone else simply falls in line with the leader. It's scary stuff!)

Guru Success Tip

Recognise that most of our communication is not through the words we speak but the way that we use our voice combined with our body language!

People tend to fall into three main categories when it comes to how they process their thinking. In the western world, the majority (about 60%) process their thinking visually (seeing their way through life), while about 30% are primarily kinesthetic (feeling their way through life) with the minority (about 10%) being audio (hearing their way through life).

But that's not all. When it comes down to communication, less than 10% of what we communicate is through the words we use. About 30% of our communication is through the way we say the words, (the tone, tempo, volume) but the majority of what we're communicating is through our body language.

Getting into rapport then, is where science meets art. How you communicate with someone (the context) is far more important than the point you're making (the content)! As well as echoing the body language and general conversational style of the other person, you can really help your cause by taking care to speak to them in their preferred thinking style, whether it's visual, audio or kinesthetic. The effects can be dramatic, as a young woman beautifully demonstrated on a training programme I once ran.

Lesley was very much a kinesthetic – she was by her own admission, very happily, the worst dressed person on the course! She had a great sense of humour, and her slow – almost deadpan delivery – made her all the more likeable. Popular with her colleagues, Lesley was big into cars. In order to demonstrate the power of language to the rest of the group, I began to talk to her about cars using visual language.

'Imagine looking at a brand new, bright red Ferrari parked outside your house. Watch as people drive past, craning their necks to get a better view of your pride and joy …' I'd continued in this vein for a while but to no avail, it was clear that Lesley just wasn't getting excited at all!

But when I switched to kinesthetic language, it was a completely different story. 'Now, I want you to imagine that you're sinking down in the Ferrari's leather seats and notice how good the sporty steering wheel feels in your hands. You've got the roof down on the car, and as you speed away from the curb, you're aware of the force of the car's acceleration and the wind in your hair …'

By this point, Lesley was almost drooling! She'd slipped down into her chair and was wearing a big smile. I could have sold her the car in an instant!

WHERE COMMUNICATION BREAKS DOWN …

Listening to the other person carefully – not only with your ears but also with your eyes – is therefore of paramount importance, whether you're looking to sell or looking for a date! Getting to grips with these rapport building skills is half the battle – but it also helps if you do your best to understand the other person first, before attempting to be understood yourself. In other words, do your best to step into the other person's map of the world.

Sadly, most people are more concerned with themselves – the 'me, me, me' society – than anyone else, little realising that this attitude only backfires. Worse, few people listen in a conversation – instead they're waiting for a gap so that they can put their next point across.

It's not hard to see that a lack of effective listening combined with mismatching and mirroring communication styles are likely to lead to poor relationships. And this is without taking into consideration whether or not either party operates with a win–win attitude! Finally, it's worth remembering that we distort our perception of the world because we're looking at it through the grey tinted lenses of our memories and experiences which are stored in the subconscious minds.

Our capacity for distorting and generalising – through our own filters of perception – can often lead to misunderstandings or a complete breakdown in communication, as two independently delightful employees of the same company had already found out to their cost …

War was beginning to break out in the branch office of one of my key clients. Apparently the office manager was constantly falling out with his secretary. People were taking sides. I'd been asked by the company's HR director if I could sort out the problem.

Interviewing the director first, I was confronted with a highly intelligent, funny and kind man – whose qualities were masked by a somewhat abrasive manner. As Peter described his secretary, it was clear that there was a major problem. From his perspective, his secretary was obstructive, unhelpful and making his life difficult. As we chatted, he told me in passing that his hobby was forensic science. Peter's language reflected his interest, and I couldn't help smiling when he'd told me at lunch time that he was so hungry, he could 'murder' a sandwich!

In the afternoon I spent some time with his secretary Sam – who to my surprise was unexpectedly gentle, helpful and loyal. I was taken aback, as in no way did she reflect the hard-faced harridan described by her boss. But, over a cup of tea, it became clear that she was experiencing major problems with Peter. I asked Sam about her goals – and what her dreams had been when she was still at school. 'I didn't really have any goals', she said, 'my school teachers didn't really take much of an interest in me.'

> **Guru Success Tip**
>
> People live up or down to your expectations – so you'll be more likely to get the results you want by being encouraging rather than critical!

I then asked Sam about her parents' aspirations for her – wondering whether they'd offered any encouragement in terms of careers advice. Sam had just looked at me blankly. A heavy silence filled the room. I could see she was going through some kind of internal battle – wondering what to say. As the quietness of the room became almost unbearable, she began to cry. Haltingly at first, Sam told me about her childhood – which had been unbearable – not least because of her father's violence.

'Nearly every night, my father knocked my mother about or picked on one of us. It got worse when he'd had too much to drink. I was the middle one of three children – and while I wanted to do all I could to save my younger sister from the same brutal treatment, I made a personal vow to leave home as soon as possible.'

But, sadly, even though she kept her vow, history was to repeat itself. Soon after leaving school, Sam met a young man called Tim and within six months they were living together. The novelty soon wore off however, when Sam discovered that Tim had an over-controlling nature and was apt to use his fists if words didn't get the response he wanted.

Suddenly, the cause of Peter and Sam's problems was crystal clear.

Peter studied forensic science and revelled in the language – Sam had experienced fear both as a child and as a young adult. Whenever Peter spoke, Sam went into an emotional panic. Cringing inwardly in fear every time words came out of his mouth, she'd learned to cope by simply tuning him out, with the result that from his perspective, she was failing to listen or carry out his instructions!

It was understandable that she felt a natural aversion to him – and the violence of his language. Now was it any wonder – not knowing her background – that Peter didn't understand why his relationship with his secretary was so bad?

Both of them agreed that they wanted to improve the situation. Sam realised that if she told Peter a little about her childhood experience, he would be intelligent enough to realise that taking the aggression out of his language would pay huge dividends. And really that was all it took to remedy the situation – helping each to understand the other's map of the world!

Finally, remember that people are doing the best they can with what they know. People who behave badly are doing so because they're in the grip of the ego, which as you now know only too well, is based in fear and illusion. I find that it helps to reframe awkward people in my mind as people who have deep issues that they're not yet ready to deal with!

Chapter 21

Using intuition and energy to create phenomenal relationships

A fter a quick lunch, in which the conversation turned to the many business applications in which what we'd learned in the morning could be applied – including the formation of effective sales relationships, managing staff and introducing change to the organisation – Pete had been equally fascinated by the potential the material held for improving life at home!

'What we've been learning about over the last two days isn't just for work, is it?' he asked, adding with a smile, 'I guess that's what makes it so interesting! I'm thinking that my wife and I could adopt some of the same approaches with our children – I wonder what would happen.'

'When you to stop to think about it, there isn't any situation in which all of this stuff couldn't be applied', Jenny added. 'After all, life is about relationships – whether it's at home, at work or when you're out socialising with your friends. It seems to me that we now have some pretty powerful tools – and it's going to be up to us to ensure that we handle them properly!'

*Listening to the delegates discuss **how** they were going to apply what they'd learned to real life was music to my ears. How often have any of us sat through interesting training courses only to leave what we've learned behind in the classroom?*

Taking our coffee back into the training room with us, we immediately embarked on the final session, to learn about intuition and working with energy! Of course, we only had time to scratch the surface – but I knew that once the delegates' appetites were whetted, they'd start to investigate the subject more thoroughly under their own steam.

After inviting the group to split into pairs, I gave one person out of each couple a piece of paper on which was written a particular feeling like 'anger' or 'sadness'.

'The idea behind this exercise is for you to see already how finely tuned your intuition is', I explained. 'For those of you with the piece of paper, I want you to remain completely still and expressionless but I want you to focus on feeling the feeling that is on your paper. If you have trouble doing this, think back to a situation in which you felt this feeling! Your partner, without talking or engaging with you in any way, is going to see what feeling they pick up from you.'

'Can't see this working', said Matt, 'but in the spirit of open-mindedness I'll give it a go!'

Silence descended upon the room as half the delegates started concentrating on their feeling, while the other half did their best to intuit what was being felt. After about a minute, I'd asked the intuiters to report back to their partners what they'd felt. It wasn't long before the sound levels in the room began to rise, as they began to realise that they were accurate in their assessment of their partner's feelings.

'Great work', I said, 'and we've only just begun! What we're going to do now is see for ourselves how, while we might think we rely on verbal communication, we don't really need it as much as you'd believe.'

Handing out some blindfolds for the next exercise, a story that illustrated the point perfectly came to mind. 'It's a long story how it came about, but a while back, I organised a trade mission to Moldova, a tiny country nestling between the Ukraine and Romania. One of the companies on the mission was interested in working with the authorities to develop the airport there – which led to a meeting between the airport directors, my client and me. With us was a Moldovan colleague acting as facilitator and interpreter. It was a good meeting and, as the directors wished to see their airport developed too, there was a shared vision and a good feeling of camaraderie.

'Two months later I caught up with the two senior directors again, this time at an airports' convention in Prague. I warned my Moldovan colleague that as he wasn't able to join us in the Czech Republic, he'd better make sure that the two directors brought an interpreter of their own, as I don't speak a work of Russian.

'"No problem" he'd said – but when the airport directors and I finally found each other at the convention, there wasn't an interpreter in sight. Clearly they'd come without one, which was adventurous to say the least! I needed to know what was happening with regard to the airport so that I could report back to my UK client – and it was clear that the directors wanted to speak with me too. So, in some inexplicable way – beyond words – we started communicating. Yes, there were a few gestures – me doing an impression of an aircraft with both my arms pointing out sideways being one of them – to help us along the way, and I'm sure the three glasses of "champanski" helped a little!

'Within five minutes, I'd gleaned all I needed to know in relation to the contract and what moves my client needed to make next. Suddenly though, I was struck by the absurdity of the situation. How could I possibly know what these two guys were thinking? I came out of our shared altered state with a thump and my confidence flew out of the window. I knew I needed to find an interpreter to verify the discussion – or at worst, to put us straight! Looking around, I spotted someone wearing a Russian name tag who was speaking English. Plucking up my courage, I went over to him and

explained that my airport directors had come with no interpreter and that we needed just five minutes of help. Very graciously, he agreed to my request – and to my utter amazement when he told me in English what the airport directors had said, it matched up perfectly with what I understood from our telepathic communication!'

'Scary stuff', laughed Matt.

'Indeed – or perhaps it's really amazing stuff!' I replied.

Having finished my story, I started to issue some instructions for the next exercise.

'OK, you'll be working with your partner once again – but this time, we're going to be working outside.' I led the way out to the beautiful gardens around the hotel and continued, 'One of you is to put on the blindfold, while the other one is going to be your guide. And yes, you'll both get the opportunity to try this out for yourselves. It's probably as well now to make a pact that you'll look after your partner and not lead them somewhere dangerous!

'For the next five minutes, I want you to go for a walk – but please remain within earshot of me. You're not allowed to talk but instead you must guide your partner through touch alone. You'll quickly come up with your own code – trust me – and you'll be amazed at just how easy you'll find it.'

Hesitantly, the delegates went off in separate directions. The blindfolded people were walking very gingerly and their guides were taking their jobs very seriously. I smiled as they did look rather strange but I knew that what they were about to experience would remove any vestiges of self-consciousness.

Soon, the trust between the couples began to develop – particularly as the blindfolded partners realised that they were safe with their guides. They began to walk a little more boldly – and more upright than before. After a couple of minutes, I called out another instruction.

'Now, I want you to continue guiding your partner, but as well as not using words, you can't use touch either. Guides, I want you to imagine that there is an energy flowing out of your hands that you can use to guide your partner. While you'll no longer be physically touching your partner, you can use the energy coming from your hands – and your intention – to guide your partner. Trust it! Have fun with it!'

Now it was the guiding partners' turn to look worried. They'd never done this before and I could almost feel their discomfort at what they were being asked to do. When I issued the fresh instruction, everyone had stopped moving. Now they started walking again, very slowly at first.

Jenny was guiding Matt and her confidence was growing by the minute. With her right hand about 18 inches behind his back and her left about a foot in front of his heart area, she proceeded to walk beside him, almost crab-like. At first they walked in a straight line but then I saw a look of horror on Jenny's face when she realised that they were walking straight towards a garden seat and that she was going to have to negotiate Matt around it – unless she was prepared to take the flack for bruising his shins!

Intuitively, she started to move from Matt's side to a point that was slightly to the side and partly to the back of him. Her right hand was in line with the back of his right shoulder while her left hand was now about six inches in front of his left shoulder but pointing in the direction she wanted him to go. To her utter amazement, he slowly started walking more towards the left. She continued in this way and managed to ensure that Matt completely missed the chair. Jenny looked relieved and then, obviously starting to enjoy herself and in a spirit of experimentation, she decided to see if she could get Matt to walk around the chair. She achieved this by moving her hands in the opposite direction, bringing her right hand around to just behind the left of his spine, again at shoulder level and her left hand in front of his chest, again facing forwards. Almost immediately, Matt slowly begun to change direction again and started walking around to the right. In this way, Jenny managed to get Matt around to the front of the chair.

Curious now as to whether she could get him to trust her enough in order to energetically persuade him to sit down – even though he didn't even know there was a chair behind him – she moved in front of him and simply stood for a couple of moments with her arms outstretched but not touching, his body. Then she began moving her hands – which were about six inches from his body – slowly downwards and at the same time she started bending her own knees, as though she too was going to sit. Imperceptibly at first, Matt began to bend his knees. He was bending forwards slightly, almost to counterbalance his weight. It was as though he was thinking about sitting – but as though he was getting ready to sit on the ground rather than on a chair!

Jenny was a natural. And judging by the experiences that the others were to later to tell us about, they too shared Jenny's abilities! It was also clear that at this stage in the course they all had an enormous amount of trust in each other – a prerequisite for being able to succeed at the exercise. When we got back to the training room, everyone was thrilled with what they'd just experienced.

'I never would have believed I could do that', said Jenny.

'No, nor would I', Matt laughed.

The others too were equally as excited by their experiences.

'So', said Pete, 'I agree that was quite remarkable. But you know me, how on earth are we going to use that in our everyday lives?'

Before I could reply, Jenny had started to speak. 'To me it's really clear. I know that I don't have to rely on just my words any more. I've seen with my own eyes that how I think – and how I intend my energy to flow – can have an amazing impact not just on a conversation but also on relationships in general. It's as though I finally understand that I have more power than I previously realised.'

Turning to me she added, as if she'd just had a revelation, 'Boy, you're right – I can see now that what you were saying yesterday really is true. If that's the power our thoughts and intentions can have, then we really do need to be careful what we spend our time thinking about!'

'Absolutely!' I replied. 'And remember, when Pete said just five times "I'm weak, I'm worthless, I'm useless," he demonstrated how much impact that negative thinking had on his body? Now, after today's exercise out in the garden, you can see just how much we communicate through the electromagnetic field that surrounds each of us.

'Intention and thoughts, as you've already seen, are incredibly powerful. And if you think back to yesterday morning, I spoke about how the subconscious mind will naturally default to the negative, unless we deliberately consciously focus on something positive – which is where having a powerful vision and SMART goals really helps.'

Aiming my next remark at Pete, I added, 'And this stuff with energy and intention really comes into play when you're seeking to create a positive outcome – whether it's in the sales arena or if you're dealing with a difficult person. I know for me, it really helps if I "set the intention" for a meeting before it starts, asking in my mind for the highest outcome for all concerned. It might sound strange, but when I've set that intention, I've been able to feel my own energy shift, almost as though it's like a heat-seeking missile searching out the win–win in a situation. When you deal with life in this way, it helps you to get out of the way of your ego as much as anything else. If you think about it, when two parties in a discussion are being driven by their egos, someone – if not both people ultimately – is going to lose.'

Slowly, the heads around the room began to nod at my words. After all they'd learned over the last couple of days – and from their in-depth one-to-one sessions with me – it was all beginning to make perfect sense.

In order to make sure that everyone really knew how to apply what they'd learned to real scenarios, I asked the delegates to provide me with a variety of scenarios that they'd had difficulty with in the past – and together, using the material we'd covered over the preceding two days, we discussed how the situations could have been better handled. They also threw into the pot some situations they were currently facing, or expected to face in the future. I was delighted to find that I was almost nothing more than an observer in the conversation – they were able to come up with all the solutions themselves!

It hadn't taken long, but now they were definitely on the path to being their own authorities, their own gurus!

As our time together was drawing to a close, I told them that I had one more really far out exercise to try – but for now I wanted to check that they had all got what they'd originally wanted out of the programme.

Going back to the flip chart, I flicked back to the first page which read:

1   Say 'no' to people

2   Manage my time better

3   Make my relationships work better

4   Make people like me

5   Manage my anger better

6   Get on in my career

7   Deal with stress

8   Avoid making the same mistakes over and over again

9   Have fun!

'OK, who said "say 'no' to people"?' I asked.

Jenny put her hand up. 'That was me!'

'Do you feel that you're better able to say "no" to people now?' I asked.

'Yes. I think that in a way, since our one-to-one session together, I feel a lot better about myself and also, because I now have goals, I'm much more focused. If someone wants me to do something that will take my eye off the ball – my ball – then I feel now as though I have the right to say "no". It's not so much that I've become hard – just more focused. Also, by creating rapport with the other person, I'll be able to say "no" in a way that doesn't make them feel that I don't care. Looking at point 2 on the list, I can also see that all I've just said is going to help me manage my time better too!'

I nodded in encouragement. 'It's funny isn't it how when you look back at the list all the items on it seem to apply to us all. So, I'll carry on down the list and if you feel that I **haven't** covered a particular point to your satisfaction then shout!'

Quickly, I went through the rest of the list. 'Do you all feel that you now know how to say "no" and manage your time better?' As I saw everyone nodding, I put a tick by points 1 and 2.

'After all that we learned with the "thinking" styles – and even the work we did with energy just now – do you feel that you know how to make your relationships work better?' Seeing the nods, I put a tick by point 3.

'Good, well in that case, you must therefore know how to get people to like you more!' Everyone laughed and I ticked point 4.

'Yesterday, we talked about the power of our emotions – and especially the detrimental effect that our negative feelings can have on us. Do you all feel confident using the PEAR model?'

Pete frowned, 'The PEAR model?'

We'd been through a lot and Pete had clearly forgotten the name of the exercise which brings about healing from anger, hurt and grief. 'Remember how you can have the conversation with someone who's hurt you, in your mind's eye …'

At that, Pete nodded and I ticked point number 5.

'Getting on in my career – can you see that by knowing how you tick, you now understand better how other people tick? If you want to get on in your career, then all you have to do is use the tools you've now acquired to manage your relationships "upwards" too! When we looked at how people process their thinking, we saw how conflicts can arise – but now you're armed with that knowledge, you can stop the problems before they start. By knowing where people are coming from, you'll know how to handle them better. And if you take the time to find out what your boss's goals and aspirations are – and do all you can to help him or her achieve them – then your place at the top is all but secured already!'

At this Pete had laughed, saying, 'Yes, all of that stuff was a real eye-opener for me. I can see how I've not got as far in my career as I'd have liked. But actually, there is something I wanted to ask you. I'm still a little concerned about that matching and mirroring of other people's behaviour because, surely, if I become more like someone else I become less like me?'

'Good point – and you should know that as I said yesterday, I really don't want you to be anything other than your real, authentic self. See if this helps – you know those large mirrored balls in nightclubs which reflect the coloured lights around the room? Well, think of yourself as the mirrored ball, the whole ball, and see yourself reflecting the little parts of yourself that echo other people's thinking, language and body styles. Does this feel right to you now?'

'Yes, it does, especially since you've put it in kinesthetic language for me!'

At this, I ticked off point number 6 on the flip chart.

'When you stop to think about it, most of our stress is caused either through the poor relationship we have with ourselves or with those we have with other people. We spent a lot of time yesterday and today understanding what makes people tick and how to improve those relationships, which in turn will help remove the causes of stress before they start.' I explained.

'Yeah, I can see exactly what you mean about relationships being the cause of a lot of our stress. But do you have any tricks for dealing with stress on the spur of the moment?'

'Indeed I do', I smiled at Matt. 'In fact, why don't you all try it right now? It's better with your eyes closed but if you have a good imagination and you find yourself somewhere where you can't close your eyes, it'll work equally as well with your eyes open! But for now, just close your eyes and imagine that you have a menthol-like bright, white light shining all around you. In a moment, I'll be asking you to breathe in three deep breaths of this beautiful white light – but I want you to breathe it in through the crown of your head, and see it lighting up each and every cell in your body before you breathe it out through the soles of your feet. So ... begin now, breathing in from that bright white light; that's right ...'

On the last breath out, Pete was the first to open his eyes again. 'Wow, that's amazing. I feel kind of refreshed – just after three breaths. I can't believe that!'

I ticked off point number 7.

'How would you avoid making the same mistakes over and over again?' I asked.

'Hmmm', said Jenny. 'I think I'm going to become much more aware – consciously – of the patterns I run in my life. If I see stuff that isn't working for me, then I'm going to try – no sorry, I can't try anymore can I – I'm going to seek the source of my negative patterns and then deal with them, using either the PEAR process or by creating goals that will simply help me bypass any unhelpful behaviours!'

'Well, I guess that means that I can also tick off point number 8, which leaves number 9, "Have fun!". I've really enjoyed my time with you – and learned a lot from you, so thank you. Have you all had fun?'

'Absolutely', came the chorus.

And with that, I ticked off point number 9.

'Before we finish up for now – and we will of course be meeting up for our personal coaching sessions over the next few months – I'd like to try an experiment with you. By now, you'll all have worked out that I have a pretty strong interest in the more esoteric side of life, and I reckon', I said, taking a candle, a two-foot high candle holder and box of matches out of my workbag, 'that if we really concentrate', I added, lighting the candle, 'we'll be able to extinguish the flame using just the power of our minds!'

Once again, they all started leaning forwards in their seats, anticipating what was coming next.

'Right, for one minute precisely, we're all going to focus our attention on the candle and imagine it going out. So, looking at the candle now … imagining the flame diminishing as you look at it … that's right, keep focusing …'

I stole a glance around the room. Each of the delegates was staring intently at the candle. Disregarding their intent totally, the candle resolutely continued to burn.

I waited exactly a minute and then called a halt to the proceedings. 'Clearly', I said in a disappointed tone, 'that's not going to work.'

'OK, Matt – will you come up to the front for me please?' As he left his seat, I added, 'Perhaps you'd like to blow out the candle for us?'

Nodding, he leaned over, and taking a deep breath he blew out the candle.

'And', I said putting my arm around him in a friendly gesture, 'as my lovely young assistant here has shown us, thinking about something isn't enough.

'To really make things happen you have to get right up … OFF YOUR BACKSIDE!' I finished in a very loud voice.

At that, they all burst out laughing and clapping at the same time! It was an apt finale to our two day session – and one that they would go on to tease each other about in the months ahead.

Points to ponder as you start to …
Be your own guru

1 Experience the power of your intuition. Working with a partner, one of you – without speaking or moving a muscle – feel an emotion, while the other intuits what that emotion is. If you find it hard to conjure up a feeling, think back to a time when you felt it for real and focus on that!

2 With a friend, try the 'communicating through energy' exercise. One of you wear a blindfold while the other guides – at first by touch and then, as you feel more comfortable, purely through your energy and intent. In your imagination, see yourself guiding your partner and consciously intend that you do so. Remember to remain focused on where you want to guide your partner – rather than on where you don't want them to go! (And it goes without saying that you should practice this exercise only with someone you trust not to put you in danger in any way!)

3 Try the deep relaxation exercise for yourself. Close your eyes and imagine that you have a warm bright, menthol-like white light all around you. Take in three deep breaths of this beautiful white light – breathing in through the crown of your head, and see it lighting up each and every cell in your body before you breathe it out through the soles of your feet.

Conclusion

The Banker announces the results for the pilot project

*N*ine months to the day after the programme had first started, The Banker called and invited me for coffee the following morning in the boardroom. 'I've got something you'll be very interested in', he said tantalisingly.

Feeling almost sick with excitement, I awoke early and made sure that I arrived in good time for our interview. Kindly, The Banker didn't keep me waiting but ushered me straight into the boardroom. 'I've asked my secretary to bring in coffee – you take yours white with no sugar; that's right isn't it?'

Surprised that he'd remembered, the man who stood before me seemed gentler somehow. I was trying to work out what was different about it him when it suddenly struck me – it was as though he was on my side for the first time. I had my fingers metaphorically crossed. While I was pleased with the way that the programme had gone – and delighted with the feedback from the delegates – I still had no idea how much it had all been translated into the only thing in which The Banker was really interested: results.

'Let me give you the headline news first', said The Banker, 'and then we can get down to the finer details. The great news is that your group improved their sales results by 330% when compared with their figures from nine months ago. That really is a pretty astonishing result! Congratulations.'

'And how did my group do in comparison with the control group?' I asked.

'A huge amount better', he laughed, 'not just in terms of sales but also they took off much less sick time than their counterparts. I'd say your programme was a resounding success all round, especially when you consider that you had the group that hadn't been performing particularly well for some time.'

He then went on to tell me that before the pilot project had begun, there had been considerable opposition not only from his colleagues but also from some of the participants.

'Some of them, particularly the older ones, were a bit cynical – I'm sure you're aware of that. But it didn't take long for you to win them over and I suspect that was because of the initial one-to-one sessions that you insisted on doing. If I'm honest, I was a bit cynical about them too. It all sounded a bit like therapy to me and I wasn't sure that they would have much effect but I have to admit that you were right to insist on doing them!'

For The Banker to admit getting something wrong was unusual, to say the least. We both knew that those sessions had been instrumental in bringing about dramatic change for nearly all those taking part. Three people had decided, after our first session together, that they didn't really want a career in banking. Two of them had already started on new careers and the third had left to return to full time education. I thought that The Banker would be annoyed but, much to my surprise, he was pleased.

'In all honesty', he said, 'I'd rather people left if they're not enjoying their work here. We all know that people are more successful when they're fired up by what they're doing and I only want passionate, keen people in my team.'

Next, we discussed the progress of the three people with whom I'd formed a particular bond.

'Jenny's come on in leaps and bounds', said The Banker. 'To look at her, you'd hardly recognise her. Apart from a new, blonde hairstyle, it's as though she's gone through a complete personal transformation! She made an appointment with me the other day and said she was looking for promotion – and wanted me to help her! At first, I was a little taken aback but then I had to admire her courage. The Jenny of old would never have said boo to a goose let alone come and boldly ask a director to champion her career progression!'

I thought back to my first meeting with Jenny and wondered if she realised just how far she'd come. Not only had her sales figures risen the most dramatically of the group but on a personal level so much had changed too. In our final coaching session, Jenny had told me that her relationship with her brother had improved so much that she and her husband regularly went out for dinner with him and his latest girlfriend. 'There's no way that I would have wanted to spend any time with him before – but ever since I went through that forgiveness exercise with you, it's as though I've been able to see him in a different light.'

Confidently, she continued, 'And the relationship with my husband is so much better too. I know that I said I was really happy with him but I'd always felt a kind of awe for him, as though he was far more important than I was. But somehow my feelings have changed – it's as though I now **know** that we're equal. And the strange thing is, the more I've taken responsibility for myself and my career, the happier we've both been! My husband admitted the other day that he'd always felt that I held him responsible for making me happy and that it was something of a burden for him. I guess that's all changed now – simply because I've changed. Thank you.' And with that, Jenny gave me a huge hug!

Pete also had seen a dramatic improvement in his own sales results. Driven by the desire to own the retirement home in France that he and his wife had always dreamed about, he'd discovered an inner drive that had surprised both him and The Banker. And his relationship with The Banker had improved too – not only because of his rapidly improving sales record but also because Pete simply knew how to handle him better!

Finally, Matt – within six months of the start of the pilot programme – was delighted with the news that he had been put up for promotion. He'd seen his sales figures sky rocket and The Banker was anxious to make Matt's career exciting enough to entice him to remain on the team rather than seek better prospects with a competitor.

As our meeting drew to a close, The Banker shook my hand and promised to write me a glowing testimonial …

Afterword

*B*e Your Own Guru* is based on a true story. While the characters Pete, Jenny and Matt are entirely fictional, their characters are based on an amalgamation of the many people (and their real life experiences) that have been through the Be Your Own Guru leadership development programme. All the anecdotal stories featured in the book are also completely true, although the names and any identifying details of the protagonists have been altered to protect their anonymity.

There's a saying that the best way to heal the world is simply to heal yourself.

It's only when we start to live our lives at 'cause' rather than 'effect' – and start to take personal responsibility for the choices that we make – that we've got a real chance to improve the way we treat ourselves, each other and the planet as a whole.

In my opinion, the world's power base currently resides in the business world. With some corporations now boasting profits that far outstrip the gross domestic product of a number of nations, it's rapidly becoming clear that our future rests no longer in the hands of the politicians but instead in the hands of the money makers. And that may be no bad thing. Most of us have to work — whether we're employed by someone else or run our own organisations. That means that we're closer to the power-brokers than we've ever been. In fact, while we may not have realised it, *we are* the power-brokers.

Organisations are nothing without their people, and people shape organisations. By waking up to our inner sense of purpose and combining this with our personal power, each and every one of us now has an invitation to play our part in creating heaven on earth!

Section Four

Tools! Tools! Tools!

Gathering knowledge isn't power – applying knowledge

is power

Tools to be your own guru

BE YOUR OWN GURU ASSESSMENT WHEELS

U se these wheels – you may like to make a regular appointment in your diary – as a personal evaluation tool to monitor your own progress as you continue your journey to becoming your own guru. (You may want to photocopy them so you have wheels for your future use. Alternatively, visit www.beyourownguru.com to download your free Be Your Own Guru toolkit.)

To use the wheels, take 1 to be the smallest, inner circle and 10 to be the largest, outer circle (the halfway line is highlighted in dark grey) mark with a cross on each vector line where you feel you are on a scale of 1 to 10. When you have completed this, join each of the crosses together, rather like a dot-to-dot exercise …

Once you've completed the wheel, it's easy to see at a glance which areas require work – and in which order! Remember, when you're travelling in a car the journey is smooth because of the round wheels on the vehicle. Any deviation from a perfect circle will therefore give us a bumpy ride through life! Perhaps surprisingly, having a perfect 10 isn't the ideal as this shows that you feel that there is no room for growth. Having a tiny but perfectly balanced wheel isn't much help either, as you'd be resigned to travelling through life pretty slowly.

Finally, because these wheels are personal to you, it's in your interests to fill them honestly. Cheat on the wheels and you cheat yourself!

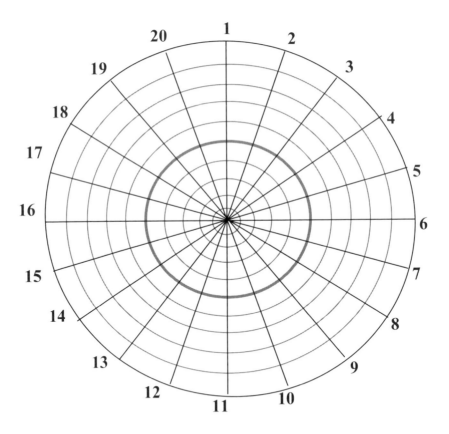

Be your own guru personal wheel

1   I understand that I am unique

2   I am comfortable with who I am and my life's purpose

3   I know that how I think and speak has a major impact on my life experience

4   I allow my intuition to guide me

5   I find it easy to say 'no' when appropriate

6   I have SMART goals (Specific, Measurable, Achievable, Ritten & Timed)

7   I don't hold grudges

8   I don't let my temper get the better of me

9   I surround myself with positive people

10   I don't let my history control my future

11   I find it easy to forgive myself

12   I am able to deal with my emotions

13   I find it easy to let go of past failures

14   I understand that in order to create successes, I need to be able to fail

15   I look after myself as though I were my best friend

16   I understand that how others see me is a reflection of who they are, not who I am

17   I allow myself 'me' time

18   I practice living in the moment rather than worrying about the future and regretting the past

19   I know that whilst I'm open to advice, I have all the answers inside me

20   I do all I can to take care of myself physically, emotionally and spiritually

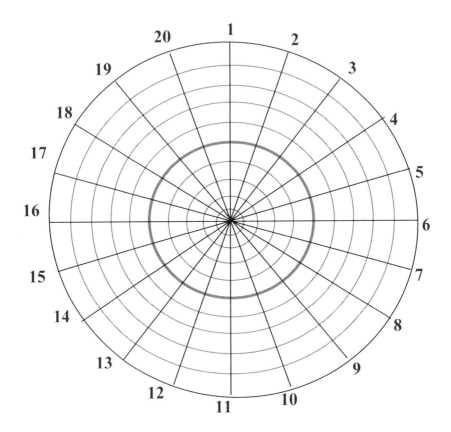

Be your own guru relationship wheel

1   My relationships are based on win–win

2   I fix myself first rather than attempt to fix others

3   I understand that everyone is doing the best they can, with what they know

4   I recognise that just because someone is different, it doesn't make them wrong

5   I really listen to others (rather than wait for an opportunity to be heard myself!)

6   I find out what's important to others and, if I can, I help them achieve their goals

7   While still being me, I do my best to speak in other people's language style

8   I understand that other people mirror what's going on within me

9   I am sensitive to others' feelings

10 I give others credit

11 I am honest with others, and don't change who I am to win their approval

12 I understand that bearing a grudge against others hurts me, not them

13 I know that forgiving others sets me free

14 I apply objectivity to my relationships

15 I give without expecting to get anything back

16 I avoid jumping to conclusions about other people's behaviour

17 I give others the benefit of the doubt

18 I honour other people's belief and value systems

19 I accept people for who they are, and don't seek to change them

20 I respect the fact that everyone has freedom of choice

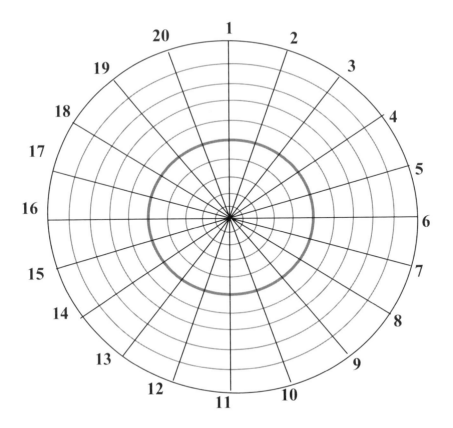

Be your own guru work wheel

1 I understand that leadership is about serving others

2 I have a clear vision of where I'm going

3 My personal goals are aligned with the expectations of my company

4 I focus on building relationships with my clients and colleagues

5 I communicate clearly at all levels

6 I know what is expected of me

7 I listen to my colleagues and take action where appropriate

8 I coach and encourage others to improve their performance and skill levels

9 I regularly give others credit for work well done

10 I support innovation and creativity in others

11 I am good at managing my time

12 I am sensitive to others' feelings

13 I am confident

14 I apply objectivity to situations

15 I like to take educated risks

16 I encourage change and flexibility

17 I analyse options from a variety of viewpoints

18 I like to gather and use information

19 I am comfortable doing presentations to others

20 I respect others for doing the best with what they know

The Self Journey
(using PEAR) *

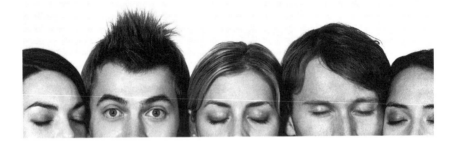

What you'll need:

- An open mind

- An hour of uninterrupted time

- A mirror

You may want to read the followings words through once or twice before beginning the exercise – or indeed record* them to guide your session. Alternatively, you may want to do the exercise with someone you trust guiding you through each step.

Look into the mirror for a few minutes, taking time to see the human being looking back at you as a 'real person'. Most of us usually look in the mirror only when we're cleaning our teeth, or grooming ourselves.

---

*   If you prefer, you can order a specially recorded 'Peeling the Pear' CD direct from www.beyourownguru.com

This means that we only see our superficial self, without getting beneath the surface. Look yourself in the eye, and really begin to get a feel for the 'you' looking back.

Now it's time to go through the PEAR process – with yourself as the protagonist!

Talk out loud to the person in the mirror, as though you're talking to a third person. It may feel a little odd at first but persevere; the results are well worth it!

1   *Expression*: Start by expressing any negativity you feel towards the person in the mirror.

'I'm so ashamed that you …' (fill in the gaps, you'll know what to say here!)

'I hate it that you …'

'I'm angry with you because …'

… and so on, you get the picture!

And then, when you think you've got it all out, ask yourself, 'What's the one thing I still haven't told you that I'm angry, ashamed or disappointed about …'

2   *Forgiveness*: Next, and this is of course ultra-important, make the decision to forgive yourself. We don't want you just to stir up the negativity and do nothing about it! Forgiveness is a decision – not something that washes over you after a certain period of time. Holding on to guilt merely holds you back – so while you'll want to make sure that you've learned the lessons you needed to learn, it's also right that you should move on. When we think badly of ourselves, we perpetuate a vicious cycle of negativity. We tend to give ourselves far harsher punishments than the courts

would ever give us – isn't it about time you showed yourself a bit of compassion?

Look yourself in the eye, and say, 'I forgive you for … and for … and for …' (fill in the blanks as appropriate) until you've been through the whole list of what makes you angry, ashamed or disappointed.

3   *Acceptance*: This time, make a decision to accept yourself as you are – and find at least five good things that you're proud of that you can tell the person in the mirror. Also tell him or her that you accept that you've not always been perfect in the past – but that you're grateful for the lessons they've taught you. And just as important, tell them that you want to set the person in the mirror free – free to be the best they can be!

4   *Love*: Imagine for a moment that you're breathing in from a huge bubble of white golden light. Know that the light is unconditional love – the love that you feel for innocent children, animals and perhaps even your family and friends. In a few moments you'll begin to know that the unconditional love is there for you too. Tell the person in the mirror that you love them! Note how difficult this may be at first … but stick with it. And notice how good you feel when you're able to look yourself in the eyes and say 'I love you'. (And don't get the sick bag out just yet … while this may sound a bit 'pink and fluffy', just know that I've taken a considerable number of company directors and senior managers through this process – and the feedback has been that the exercise was tremendously and profoundly powerful!)

5   *Letting go*: Just decide – and tell the person in the mirror – that you're grateful to him or her for bringing you to this point today and that you happily decide to the let the 'you' of the past go. Now make the decision to welcome in the 'you' of the future, the you that can live to his or her full potential.

The Relationship Journey (using PEAR) *

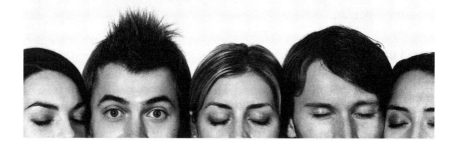

What you'll need:

- An open mind

- An hour of uninterrupted time

You may want to read the followings words through once or twice before beginning the exercise – or indeed record* them to guide your session. Alternatively, you may want to do the exercise with someone you trust guiding you through each step.

As you know, your subconscious mind doesn't distinguish between vivid imagination and reality, which is why this exercise works without you having to hold the conversation in reality. While you'll be doing this exercise in your mind – to make it more realistic, have the conversation out loud.

---

*   If you prefer, you can order a specially recorded 'Peeling the Pear' CD direct from www.beyourownguru.com

In your imagination, conjure up an image of the person with whom you're feeling angry, disappointed or hurt. To help make it very vivid, imagine what they're wearing.

Speaking out loud, but seeing events in your mind's eye, invite the other person to take a seat. Say their name and ask them to listen to you, without interrupting.

1   *Expression*: Start by expressing any negativity you feel towards the other person.

'I'm so angry that you …' (fill in the gaps, you'll know what to say here!)

'I hate it that you …'

'I'm hurt that you …'

Tell them. And then, when you think you've got it all out, ask yourself, 'What's the one thing I still haven't told the other person that I'm angry, ashamed or disappointed about …' Then proceed to tell them about that too!

2   *Forgiveness*: Next, and this is of course ultra-important, make the decision to forgive the other person for each and every transgression. Remember, forgiveness is a decision – not something that washes over you after a certain period of time. Holding on to your anger merely hurts you – not the other person! Forgiveness doesn't mean that you condone the other person's behaviour but it is the key to your happiness and freedom.

In your imagination, look at the other person and say, 'I forgive you for … and for … and for …' (fill in the blanks as appropriate) until you've been through the whole list of what makes you angry, ashamed or disappointed. You may find it easier to start with something small and work up to the really big issues.

3   *Acceptance*: This time, make a decision to accept the other person as they are. Know that how you feel about them doesn't change who they are – and remember that we're all doing the best we can with what we know. You may also find it easier to distinguish people – and who they are at their core – from their behaviours. Know also that the other person may never change, but by making the decisions that you have, you've changed. We can never change another person, only ourselves. However, once you change, the dynamics of your relationships change – and that's when seeming miracles start to happen!

4   *Love*: Choose to tell the other person that you love them – unconditionally. You might find it easier to make this statement when you think about speaking from your soul rather than your ego. Imagine – whether or not you would do so in real life – giving the other person a hug. Notice that you're able to do this because through the decisions you've made, you're now stronger and more powerful within yourself. Feel how good it is to be at 'cause' rather than 'effect' in the relationship. You may also at this point decide to give the other person a gift. What is it? What does this mean to you?

    You may also ask the other person if they have a gift for you. What is it? Is it symbolic or something that's personal to you? If there's nothing, you might like to think about what 'freedom', 'happiness' and 'potential' look like! They look like nothing too. Which of these three gifts do you think the other person would want to give to you?

5   *Letting go*: Thank the other person for their time and for listening to all that you had to say – and tell them that it's now time for them to go. Watch as they nod their head and start walking towards the door that you're able to see in your imagination. As they reach the door, they turn round to look at you one last time. Smile at the person and say 'It really is time for you to go now … and know that you go with my blessing.' Watch as the other person disappears from view.

Spend a couple of moments on your own, contemplating the great gift that you have given the other person – your forgiveness. Also think about what you've received – your freedom, happiness and the ability to live up to your full potential.

Imagine a bright white light with golden flecks all around you. Begin to breath in this white light through the crown of your head and down into each and every cell of your body. Imagine it cleansing, healing and bringing your body into balance. Breathe out through the soles of your feet. Do at least three of these deep breaths from the white, golden light. (You can also use this breathing exercise any time when you feel stressed – at work, in a traffic jam or even to help you to sleep at night!)

The Soul Journey *

What you'll need:

- An open mind

- An hour of uninterrupted time

You may want to read the followings words through once or twice before beginning the exercise – or indeed record* them to guide your session. Alternatively, simply read through the narrative and see where your imagination takes you, or do the exercise with someone you trust guiding you through each step.

Imagine that you have a beautiful bright white light surrounding you and breathe in from that light, imagining that you are breathing in through the crown of your head and out through the soles of your feet.

---

*   If you prefer, you can order a specially recorded 'Soul Journey' CD direct from www.beyourownguru.com

You will feel yourself starting to become more relaxed, and as you read the words that follow, you allow yourself to daydream …

You decide to fast forward the movie that is your life, and easily find the point – in many years' time – in which your funeral is taking place. Much to your relief and joy, you begin to realise that your funeral doesn't signify the end of you, but only the body that you have known in this lifetime. It's as though you realise, maybe for the first time, that your essence is eternal.

As you float among the mourners at your funeral, you're aware that you can see and hear what's going on. It's as though you're really there but with one difference: no one else is aware of your presence.

You look around – how many people have come to your funeral? Are you disappointed with the turnout, or surprised by just how many people have turned up? You see members of your family and your close friends and begin to feel their emotions. You find yourself able to listen in on their conversations. Are they saying that yours was a life well-lived? Are they full of admiration for you because you made the most of every precious moment, seeking as many experiences as possible – or are they saying it was a shame that you felt you had to conform in a bid to avoid your family and friends' disapproval?

Someone stands up to deliver your eulogy – who is it and what do they say? Do they talk about your warmth, humour and vitality – or are the gathered mourners just treated to a list of your scholastic, professional and perhaps sporting accomplishments? As you listen, do you feel that your life has been exciting and colourful or 'correct' and colourless?

And you notice on one of the seats that someone has folded a news-paper page to reveal your obituary. You begin to read it – what does it say? What would you have liked it to say? If you had the chance to write your obituary, how would it read? You smile inwardly as you remember the remark that, on their deathbeds, nobody ever says that they wished they'd attended more meetings! You begin to remember the things in life that brought you great joy – together with the things in life that you worried about, but which never happened.

If you were to be given a second chance to do things differently, what would you change? What would you do more of – and what time wasting things would you eliminate?

You remember all that you've learned on your journey into the future and as you start to come back into the present, you pick up your pen and paper and begin to write about the insights you've received.

Index

action plans 102–5
anger
    dealing with 42
    expressing 73–4, 115
    and health/illness 40–43
    holding on to 40
assessment wheels 211–12
    guru work 21617
    personal 212–13
    relationship 214–15
audio people 17–18, 174–5, 184
auditory digital 176

belief systems 109–10
blaming others 160–61

careers
    finding own path 15–16
    interest in other people 13–14
    success in 14–15
    target-setting 45–9

comfort zone 153–5
communication 185–8

death 143–5
    facing 151–6
    fear of 151–2
    life in comfort zone 153–5
    spiritual choice 155–6
decision making 155–6

ego
    belief in self 169
    feeling of separateness 166–7
    formation 166
    growing up 167–9
    role of 159–60, 165
    self importance/self-worth 182
    and world of duality 165–6
emotional intelligence
    concept 67–9
    role 69

emotional security 145
emotions
    anger 40–43
    fear 38
    guilt 39–40
    negative 33–4, 64–6, 69–72
    power of 66–7
    rejection 43–4
empowerment 122, 207–8
energy flow 193–6

fear 145
    of disappointment 106
    of failure 154–5
    imaginative 38
    reality-based 38
    of rejection 43–4
forgiveness 118, 139
    as healer 74
    of others 25–30, 59–61
    of self 74, 76–7
free will 164–5
Freud, Sigmund 91

goal setting 45–9, 54–5
    action plan 55–6, 102–5
    magic of 101–2
    SMART 55–7, 94–7
    visualisation 57, 100–101
guilt 39–40

Hill, Napoleon 86

influence 178
inner voice 136–7
    affirmation/commitment 141–2
    beliefs/experiences 137–9
    judging/comparing 127
    subconscious influence 139–42
    trying to do something 140–41
intuition 189–201

Jung, Carl 180

karma 109
kinesiology 121–2, 130–34
kinesthetics 175–6, 178, 184–5

listening 185–8

manipulation 178
mind/body connection 86, 114–19
    kinesiology 121–2, 130–34
    placebo effect 123
    shaman magic 123–6
    symbolism 126–8

Nasrudin, Mullah 160
negative people 16
negativity 111–12
    dealing with 42, 64
    as default thinking 98–9
    dissociation from 132
    emotional 33–4
    health/illness 113
    as hurtful to self 64–6
    letting go 100
    letting go of 69–72
Neuro-Linguistic Programming (NLP)
    181, 183

PEAR (Personal Enlightenment and
    Release) 70–72, 116, 127, 139
    acceptance 74, 220
    expressing anger, grief, hurt 73–4,
    219
    forgiveness 74, 219–20
    letting go 75, 220
    love 75, 220
    process 75–6
    relationships 21–4
    using on self 76–7

people development
   and Chinese medicine analogy 4
   failure of 12
   and groupie mentality 5
   and personal leadership 4
   as waste of time 3–4
people pleasing 23–5
perceptions 93
personal development
   control over own life 18
   dumping personal baggage 25–30
   habits/motivation 17
   understanding why you do what you
      do 17–18
personal life purpose 13, 15–16
personal responsibility 23
personality 180–81
placebo 123
positive attitude 155

Reiki 124–5
rejection 43–4
relationships
   communication 185–8
   creating effective 181–5
   establishing rapport 183–5
   PEAR process 221–4

self love 116, 182
   being good enough 35–7
   facing the past 34, 37
   and forgiveness of others 25–30,
      59–61
   and negative emotions 33–4
   reasons for disliking self 37–44
SMART goals 55–7, 94–7, 100, 101–2,
   195
soul journey 146–9, 157–8, 225–7
Sperry, Roger W. 89–90
spiritual world 166

stress
   dealing with 51–3
   distress/eustress 50–51
subconscious 67
   getting to grips with belief systems
      109–10
   goals 94–7
   iceberg representation 91
   influence of 139–42
   information filter 92–3
   left/right brain thinking 89–90
   making effective action plan 102–5
   master/slave analogy 93
   power of 62, 83–6, 113
   powers of visualisation 105–9
   prime objectives 92
   re-programming 100–102
   SMART goal setting 101–2
   and survival 90–91
   taking the strain 98–102
   tuning out 98
   as visual 93
symbolism 126–8

thinking types 174–8
training 9
   delegates 10
   focus on strengths 16–17
   improving skills 17
   one size fits all 16
   programme outline 10–11
   results of piolt project 203–6
   testing programme 1–3
trust 117, 182, 192, 194

visual people 174, 175, 177–8, 184
visualisation 105–9

wheel of life 19–23
   instructions for 31–2